THE GREEN EDIT

TRAVEL

EBURY
PRESS

TRAVEL

Easy tips for the eco-friendly traveller

JULIET KINSMAN

CONTENTS

INTRODUCTION

I once heard someone compare
sustainability to teenage sex ...
Everyone's talking about it,
very few are actually doing it,
and those that are doing it
aren't doing it very well.

Thankfully, that's changing. There's more walk; it's not all talk. Green travel no longer means having to scrimp on comfort or joy – in many ways, it's about experiencing travel in a more enriching way; a more authentic, tactile, edifying, soul-tickling way. Being green has never been so gratifying.

Obviously, the shorter the distance we stray from home, the lower our carbon footprint, but when it comes to far-flung forays there are lots of destinations that need more tourism, too. For me, being 'green' isn't just about being kind to the environment, but about getting back to how nature intended time to be spent. This, we've learned in recent times, is now more important than ever. From aviation to accommodation to carbon offsetting and 'undertourism' (see page 34), this book will help you understand every link in the travel chain, so you can choose wisely and let your travels be a force for good.

In an era where we've become addicted to convenience, instant gratification and disposability, we can feel paralysed, as though all the world's challenges are too daunting and insurmountable. I hope that reading this book will make things feel a lot easier. Here, I recommend small changes that can make a big difference when planning your trips near and far, with helpful signposts on where to go, hacks on what to pack and secrets that will help you organise how to get anywhere.

Back in 1900, Leo Tolstoy said, 'Everyone thinks of changing the world, but no one thinks of changing himself.' Maybe by the end of this decade, we'll remember the 2020s as the decade when 'sustainability' became more than an on-trend, overused buzzword and instead the start of a new era that saw us change our ways.

"

It's never been more rewarding
to feel you're having a positive
impact, while also having the best
possible holiday.

"

MY STORY

I've been a journalist for two and a half decades, and I've spent most of this time writing about hotels and luxury travel. As much as I loved all the five-star stays, the excess and indulgence never sat right with me. As dreamy as it sounds to be able to call flying around the globe and staying in world-class hotels 'work', there was always a nagging guilt. So I started this new decade determined to think of it as the Restoring Twenties – a time when everyone finally joins the conversation about sustainability and wakes up to what can be done when we're more responsible travellers who care about effecting social change.

Originally a music journalist, I began my career as a hotel specialist when my friends had an idea for a hotel guide for folks who wanted to get their weekend escapes right every time. We created Mr & Mrs Smith – an authoritative travel brand with an uplifting and irreverent voice. The first book we published was a bestseller, so great was the appetite for finding the best boutique hotels. After many years as editor-in-chief, I started to notice that some of the hotels we really loved warranted a recommendation for more than just their style – they were doing that bit more for the environment or their communities.

To spotlight these heroes, I created Bouteco.co and started working with hotels that stand for something and deserve to stand out for it. My platform helps hotel lovers find the best eco-conscious design-led hotels and I work with hoteliers to improve their sustainability, social responsibility and communications so that discerning travellers can make informed decisions. I believe that the more we talk about sustainability and what's good for the guest, good for the hotels and good for the world, the more we all benefit. And now, with this book, I aim to pass a little more of that knowledge on to you, with tips on how to make your own personal actions as a traveller more eco-conscious.

66

I believe that the more we talk about sustainability and what's good for the guest, good for the hotels and good for the world, the more we all benefit.

99

NAVIGATING OUR CHOICES

Let's inspire each other to understand better how our actions can pay it forward.

'Green' needn't mean going full hippy or horticulturalist; it means having a better understanding of the supply chains and navigating choices with more consideration and making the 'right' decision as a savvy, switched-on economist, ecologist, anthropologist, sociologist, philosopher, scientist – or half-decent person.

It's time to snap out of autopilot and enjoy the process of taking a little more responsibility when it comes to making low-carbon, low-impact choices. Look to the Slow Food Movement for a great model of celebrating local, seasonal sourcing and the pleasures of simple, quality cooking. Just as we've woken up to the harms caused by industrial agriculture and international freighting, and the destructive nature of fast fashion with its toxic dyes, resource-guzzling and child-labour abuses, it's time to get our heads around the same values in travel. Cultivating an appreciation for companies with purpose-driven policies is fantastically gratifying.

> Just as the places we visit are a mirror reflecting our curiosity, everything we do and where we choose to spend money reflects our values and our hopes for the future.

It's amazing how quickly revolutions can happen – just think of the public attitude towards plastic after David Attenborough's *Blue Planet* broadcast. Since 80 per cent of any purchase made is emotional, let's follow our hearts. By committing to something better, we're already part of a huge shift. Deep down, most humans want do the right thing, if they can – especially if they're truly aware of the wider implications of each decision. The problem is that the effect of our actions can feel intangible – as though it's a drop in the ocean. But each drop has a ripple effect. Even if you only take on board one or two tips from this book, just those could make a difference to a family somewhere soon, and countless of their relatives in the future.

My motto
is always this:
stop, think,
discuss.

Every single time we make a decision, about anything, we are essentially taking a vote for the world we want to live in. Pause. Ponder. Dig deeper. Then act.

Let's keep assessing our holiday options. You don't need me to tell you that big, international, all-inclusive resorts and cruises are not the best option from an eco-friendly standpoint ... but I'm not here to lecture you. As we've seen, the landscape is also constantly evolving, so I want to arm you with the information you need to make more informed, greener choices, as well as give you some great tips on how to plan your next trip.

So, let's crack on and make memories that give us a tingle whenever we think of them; recollections that aren't just enriching in photo albums or social feeds, but help us all to have a legacy. I want this guide to inspire you to plan the best possible trips, so that you can see incredible places, meet interesting people and improve the lives of many others along the way — and for future generations.

WE NEED TO TALK ABOUT CARBON

Understanding the carbon cycle, and in particular what that means in terms of our own carbon footprint, is one of the best ways to appreciate the impact and the sustainability of our actions (see also the Glossary, page 126).

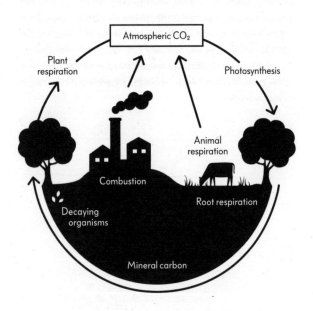

Carbon is one of the most ubiquitous elements, which is found all around us in different forms with different functions – its molecules are constantly shape-shifting and resizing, transferring from one system to another, from solid to air, in and around our planet. Much of what is living – people, plants, animals, trees, soil – is a composite of carbon, and this is thanks to microorganisms that break down dead matter, organisms and the environment trade particles, releasing carbon into the atmosphere or retaining it in the earth. Carbon sparkles in the form of diamonds, but it is vilified in its polluting gas form – or 'greenhouse gases'.

Carbon existing in wood and fossil fuels is just fine, but burning them to create energy and therefore release excess carbon into the atmosphere as carbon dioxide is where we have a problem, because it upsets the delicate carbon balance of the atmosphere. Our personal carbon 'footprints', which are measured in tonnes, refer to the total amount of greenhouse gases generated as the result of our activity.

The way to balance these carbon emissions is by increasing what is known as 'drawdown'. This is when greenhouse gases are literally drawn down towards the earth, which is done by trees and plants as they absorb carbon dioxide during photosynthesis. That is why deforestation is such a damaging contributor to global warming and why we need to preserve our tropical forests and thriving coastal habitats, such as mangroves, marshes and seagrass beds (which incidentally sequester up to 40 times more carbon than rainforests). Peaty soils are strong carbon stores that are fast being oxidised (carbon + oxygen = carbon dioxide) through deforestation, burning, farming and mining.

By restoring health to the earth
we allow natural vegetation to
recover, enabling better drainage,
which helps suck back much of
the carbon that has been released
into the atmosphere.

A robust feedback loop means there isn't just one-way traffic of carbon being converted into gas.

How does this biology lesson help us to travel more sustainably? Hopefully it shows you how important it is to support airlines which invest in and use renewable energy to reduce emissions, to choose a hotel that is actively working to reduce its carbon footprint, and to travel to places that are investing in conservation and boosting biodiversity. When we talk about wildlife and nature conservation it is the planned management of wild species, their habitats, the landscapes they live within, and making sure those ecosystems are conserved, maintained and enhanced as well encouraging healthy soil formation and preservation of natural resources.

One of the mind-broadening, perspective-enriching aspects of exploring this Earth of ours is meeting people with contrasting world views.

THE ART
OF GENTLE
PROSELYTISING

When encouraging others to be greener, it's best to master the art of gentle proselytising, in the way that a parent might coax their child to reach a conclusion on their own rather than lecturing others or making them feel as if they're being scolded. Everyone is entitled to their own take on a topic, but it's worth remembering that there is a lot of misinformation and conjecture masquerading as fact floating around out there. So if you think someone you know needs their eyes opening to a greener way of life, it is of course important to do what you can to help, but there are good and bad ways to go about this.

Shaming tactics aren't ideal – they make you sound superior. A longer-term approach is to help others understand how adjusting their behaviour might also benefit their own lifestyle. Listen a lot, too – be more on receive than send. When it comes to communicating a sense of urgency, it can be hard for people to connect with large-scale change that they can't see in front of them in micro form. It's difficult to grasp situations that haven't happened yet, such as the macro outcome of climate change. Although the recent unprecedented pause on travel during the COVID-19 pandemic may help in the long term, as we've seen how quickly nature can recover if it is given a chance.

One of the mind-broadening, perspective-enriching aspects of exploring this Earth of ours through travelling is meeting people with contrasting world views. But it's not just global temperatures that are quick to rise – touching upon topics such as climate change can see conversations get heated. We can't expect to change everyone's mindset around the importance of being greener, but rock-solid facts and stats do help when speaking to those who are swayed by science rather than emotive anecdotes.

Understanding how and why carbon and climate change are connected can be what convinces. Or providing effective examples of the impact of the behaviour of developed countries on less-privileged communities. In Bangladesh, for example, despite contributing less than 0.5 per cent of global greenhouse gases, 700,000 citizens have been displaced in the last decade as a result of the floods and droughts caused by climate change, a number which is estimated could rise to 13.3 million by 2050.

DAILY TRAVEL

Though this book largely deals with travelling for leisure, many of us are on the move daily – over short or long distances – so it's worth having a quick look at the impact on the environment of our chosen method of everyday travel.

Walking

It's free, it's good for you, it's good for the environment. Get into the habit of walking wherever and whenever you can, and allowing extra time to get to places on foot, and you may find it's about a lot more than just getting from A to B. It's like bipedal meditation. Listen to music or podcasts, or look at the biological benefits to blood pressure, bone density and fitness levels.

Thankfully we're now more aware of the walkability of our cities than ever, which has meant an increase in pedestrian-friendly routes. If you need a good motivator, aim to get 10,000 steps in a day by tracking on your smartphone how much you're walking, and you could see yourself getting into better shape than ever.

Cycling

Human-powered transit is always a winner, and many forward-looking cities have paved the way with cyclescape schemes and widely available bike-hiring services. Safer routes are being rolled out across all major urban hubs in response to the spike in commuters and tourists keen to get around, al fresco. Dockless cycle hire is also on the up, with e-bikes for those wanting a little help. For those who don't live in cities and don't own a bicycle, lots of companies support the Cycle-to-Work scheme, which means you can buy a bike without having to pay anything upfront; instead the payments come out of your salary over a 12-month period.

Trains and buses

Public transit is obviously the greener option as it allows lots of passengers to get around in one vehicle rather than lots of small vehicles – be it train, bus or tram – thereby reducing emissions and congestion in urban areas. Improvements in fuel efficiency and diesel power also mean the average amount of energy used for every passenger is ever decreasing. Riding double-decker buses is one of the best ways to see many cities, too – and it feels better now that many of the buses which ran on pure diesel have been phased out. If the distance you need to traverse is just too far, the good news is modern coaches are more comfortable and better maintained than ever with extended legroom and DVD players. Fewer vehicles on the roads also means less need for nature preserves or parkland to be surrendered for more carriageways.

Riverboats

If your route allows for hopping aboard a boat, travelling by water is always a tonic. As an example, London's Thames Clipper river taxi service is an undersung mode of transport and treats you to views of the Houses of Parliament, the London Eye, St Paul's Cathedral, Shakespeare's Globe Theatre, the Tower of London and Tower Bridge. Liverpudlian commuters who live in the Wirral have the Mersey Ferry to scoot them from Seacombe and Birkenhead in a way that would make Gerry & The Pacemakers proud.

Cars

For some of us, travelling by car really is the only available option. If that's the case, consider joining a car club. It's estimated that for every membership, 14 cars are taken off the road. Enrolling in a club helps reduce congestion, improves air quality, and is an excellent cost-cutter – as most sustainability tips usually are. If you're not squeamish about sharing your space with a stranger, seek out ride-sharing opportunities through dedicated websites, such as BlaBlaCar or Liftshare. The rise of taxi apps such as Uber have clogged our roads once more. If you really need to hop in a taxi, at least choose a zero-emissions option.

HOLIDAY
PLANNING

CHAPTER 1

So, first things first: where and when to go?

The first stage of our wanderlust wonderings can be the most powerful when it comes to weighing up our impact. Psychologists say that the getting ready to go bit is almost as fun as the going. The anticipation of heading off on holiday releases endorphins that lift our mood – so imagine how you'll feel if you've invested time in making it extra sustainable? That buzz is going to be even greater, surely?

DECIDING
WHERE TO GO

*When deciding where to travel to there are
a couple of factors to consider in order to
maximise our positive impact.*

Perhaps the more obvious of the two is choosing somewhere that you don't have to fly to, which I cover in more detail in the **How to get there** section (see page 42).

The second factor is what part tourism plays in that destination's ecosystem – there are definitely some places in the world that need us more than others. Countries and regions most dependent on tourism, where the money you spend stays in local hands, are good to prioritise. At the same time, places that have seen the effects of tourism pollute or destroy their precious biodiversity (for example, the Great Barrier Reef) are best steered clear of. It may be that putting more thought into where you travel to opens your world to new and exciting places you might not have seen otherwise. Rewiring our brains to explore unexpected avenues is what green travel is all about.

Some countries even invite you to sign a voluntary 'eco pledge' to be good environmental stewards for the duration of your stay with them. The island nation of Palau in the Pacific was the first to mandate this with a stamp in your passport.

What makes a destination
more sustainable?

Think about what matters to you and what your values are, then choose a country that reflects this, or where you feel you can help make a positive difference. There are lots of ways to judge how much a nation's halo shines. Choosing a destination with a heart and head for sustainability and conservation is one way to steer yourself to greener getaways. Northern European nations – particularly Sweden, Norway and Denmark, as well as Finland, Iceland, Switzerland and Holland – usually top the league tables of goody-goodies when it comes to the environment. Here are some other examples of destinations that are worth considering:

1. **Venezuela.** If you care how much land a nation protects, Venezuela (despite its political instability) leads the way. More than half of this South American country is national parkland or a UNESCO World Heritage-protected biosphere reserve.

2. **Slovenia.** It may be small, but this central European country with its chocolate-box mountain scenery and medieval fairytale villages punches above its weight in the land conservation stakes, with about 10 per cent of its rolling countryside formally protected.

3. **Bhutan.** Time spent in this Buddhist kingdom in the Himalayas is humbling. Punctuated by emerald-green forests and glacial valleys, it's hard not to be in constant awe of a rural nation that has stayed true to its environment while immersing visiting guests in an authentic way of living. As tourism is so regulated here, those that do pay the premium to come are welcomed into their compassionate culture and inclusive community, with few barriers between the Bhutanese and foreign visitors.

4. **Cambodia**. Despite its recent history of being less than liberal, Cambodia is worth considering thanks to the incredible charity work of some of the hotels. Designer Bill Bensley's hotel group, Shinta Mani, supports a hospitality training school that educates students from disadvantaged backgrounds and supports their families. The non-governmental organisation (NGO), Room to Read, helps Cambodian girls continue their secondary school education in Siem Reap; with Rosewood Hotels being one benefactor.

5. Scotland. To reconnect with the wilderness, swathes of Scottish land are being rewilded thanks to the efforts of The European Nature Trust (TENT). They remind us that spending time in nature is good for mental health and stress relief, physical wellness and development in childhood. TENT also host experiences, which in return fund their conservation projects on the ground. In Romania, TENT is helping to create what will be Europe's largest forested protected area in the Carpathian Mountains; they hope it will become the Yellowstone Park of Europe.

6. Namibia is the first African nation to write protection of the environment into its constitution. Yes, that can mean safari adventures here can be pretty pricey, but if you're prepared to pay it forward, consult The Long Run (see opposite) to see which hotels and resorts are doing this kind of thing best.

THE LONG RUN

Originally founded by Jochen Zeitz, this non-profit organisation is a membership group of nature-based tourism businesses committed to promoting sustainability. Having merged with NEPCon, they're aiming to be the world's largest private nature conservation association, defining approaches and policies that drive conservation and community wellbeing in the long term. Through their membership, hotels and resorts learn how to integrate sustainability into all business decisions, potentially with the aim of being named Global Ecosphere Retreats (GERs). Their 4C framework considers Conservation, Community, Culture and Commerce — because without revenue you can't do the good work. Today, The Long Run members protect millions of acres of nature and hundreds of endangered or threatened wildlife species, and their work touches the lives of hundreds of thousands of people.

Undertourism and disaster tourism – trips that make a difference

Disaster tourism is a less obvious way to make your trip count. Don't be deceived by the negative-sounding nature of this, what it actually describes is the practice of visiting locations that have been victims of an environmental disaster, either natural or man-made. As an example, the start of this decade marked the fifth anniversary of the devastating Nepal earthquake. As with many other re-covering destinations, such as tsunami- and terrorism-hit Sri Lanka, communities are not only impacted by the devastation of the natural disaster or an attack, but their economy is decimated by the ensuing drop in tourism income. Visiting them is the obvious antidote. Of course, the situation is nuanced, so make a call at your precise time of booking. A destination that may have once been over-popularised, is as a result utterly dependent on tour-ism and devastated when that traffic drops: if you think your positive impact outweighs the negative, it could be the right call.

> Seeking out places that really
> need us, where they would benefit
> from having more visitors, is
> a phenomenon also known as
> undertourism.

It is a status that shifts and changes according to popularity or circumstances. Bhutan's 'low-volume, high-value' policy has helped the country thrive through a less-is-more approach to tourism, so their undertourism is deliberate. Or seek out untrammelled paths to UNESCO-protected paradises such as Costa Rica, where mass tourism hasn't yet hit, and a paucity of other travellers is part of the appeal. Australia experienced significant undertourism following the bushfires. While bushfires are not unusual, the difference this time was the scale, the impact and intensity of them, in New South Wales and Victoria in particular. A significant way to support such affected areas would be by booking a holiday off-season with a hotel or tour operator that has strong links to conservation in an area of the country suffering from the reduced number of visitors, but not impacted by the fires.

Staycations

In recent times we've had to slow down and take a longer look at what's right in front of us, so now is the time to get out and see all those corners of your homeland that you've neglected to visit. Staycations, depending on where you live, have pros and cons, just like anything, but there is no denying that from an environmental standpoint, it's one of the greenest options available to you. In the British Isles, it was a desire for guaranteed sunshine that led us to loungers by the pools and to head off to cheap-and-cheerful Spanish resorts care of bargain package holidays, and though we're still not assured of sun in the UK summer, you could argue that, thanks to climate change, the weather is now fairly reliably unreliable universally. If you're prepared to be pragmatic and easy-going about the weather forecast, the most headache-free, relaxing and sustainable option is often to holiday at home.

"

In the case of the United Kingdom, there's culture, coastline, conservation parks and countryside aplenty.

"

Places to discover in Britain:

1. Parts of the Isles of Scilly off the Cornish coast look like the Caribbean, with azure waters and white sandy beaches. Let Devon and Dorset's Jurassic Coast lure you to go fossil hunting along its 95-mile stretch of cliffs and beaches.

2. Culture-rich city breaks in Glasgow, Liverpool, York, Harrogate, Manchester, Bristol or Bath have often made me wonder why anyone ever bothers with a passport. Castles, gardens, galleries, Michelin-starred restaurants – we've got all of them in spades ...

3. Pack up your bucket and spade and head to Holkham or Wells-next-the-Sea in Norfolk, or Camber Sands or Broadstairs' Botany Bay in Kent for eye-popping panoramas of soft sandy beaches. Or you could trace the 870-mile-long Wales Coast Path which spans 70 beaches, 15 ports and secret coves galore from Chepstow in the south to Queensferry, Flintshire, in the north. Surfing families, get thee to Scotland's east-facing Lunan Bay.

4. Enjoy stepping back in time with a whirl on an island such as the Isle of Wight, car-free Eilean Shona off the west coast of Scotland or miniscule Mersea in an Essex estuary.

5. Grab your walking boots and sidestep the obvious circuits of the Lake District or Yorkshire Dales in favour of the beautiful forests and rolling countryside of Bowland in Lancashire and the Yorkshire Wolds.

What to avoid

When it comes to where not to go, you may choose to steer yourselves away from anywhere with a bad humanitarian reputation. Should we visit destinations with notoriously oppressive regimes? It's a moral dilemma. And will the money that we spend in that place benefit its citizens or only those in charge? The counterargument for this is that by visiting somewhere criticised for its lack of democracy, you may also be a small part of its eventual journey to progress.

Overtourism is another factor to consider when thinking about where to go. Aside from the obvious detractors of long queues and overpriced restaurants, overpopular destinations often score low in the sustainability stakes. This can be due to many reasons, such as holiday rentals driving prices up so locals have no choice but to move away, busy roads jammed with visitors, wildlife being scared away by the crowds – the list goes on. If you insist on visiting the big-hitters, it's smarter, at least, to schedule your trip for off-season.

It might be helpful to envisage what you want from your trip and picture the poster destination for that, then come up with its 'twin' destination, which is a lesser-known counterpart. Here are some ideas to get you started:

If you've always wanted to go to …	Instead try …
Machu Picchu, Peru	Kuélap, Peru
Venice, Italy	Treviso, Italy
Mount Everest, Nepal	Ladakh, India
Iceland	Faroe Islands, Denmark
Provence, France	The Lot or Gers, France
Bali, Indonesia	Karimunjawa, off Java
Chiang Mai, Thailand	Nan, Thailand
Algarve, Portugal	Comporta, Portugal
Santorini, Greece	Hydra or Ithaka, Greece
Uluru, Northern Territory, National Park, South Australia	Wilpena Pound, Flinders Ranges National Park, South Australia

A final word on overtourism: remember that things can change, and quickly. Even the busiest of holiday destinations, in the blink of an eye — due to political or social unrest, a natural disaster or a pandemic — can lose all their visitors, so keep up with changing situations as best you can. You can check government advice on travel to particular countries before deciding where to go.

DECIDING WHEN TO TRAVEL

A good rule of thumb when it comes to value and sustainability is to avoid going to your chosen destination at its most popular time.

Travelling in shoulder season (before and after the peak) is not only going to be better priced but can be the more sustainable option because you're not adding to the rush-hour impact. Off-season might be better in terms of jostling with fewer people anyway, and it helps provide much-needed income to locals when there are fewer tourists.

It might be rainy, colder or have darker days then, and therefore not as appealing for your precious leisure time, but sometimes the seasons that don't grab the top headlines have their own virtues. Spring may be chilly, but do some reading up and you might find it presents a rare chance to see rolling hills carpeted with wildflowers. Summer in tropical regions could be too wet for some, but ask a photographer about the spells between showers and they may tell you it's a lush, dewy dream. Autumn some might extol for its mild, dry weather ideal for hiking and biking. Beachy coastlines aren't an obvious choice in deep winter, but an in-the-know travel agent could reveal they're the perfect spot to look up from for spectacular starscapes.

I've loved spending time in European ski resorts in summer where warm days are perfect for trekking, and there are not many experiences for me that beat a dip in an alpine freshwater lake surrounded by green fields at the foot of snow-dusted summits.

Consulting travel experts, either through reading newspaper or magazine articles or by speaking to dedicated specialists about the nuances of when to go where will help you carve out a less stereotypical sojourn. Obviously, many of us are slaves to the school holidays, so there's less flexibility. But if you want to help mitigate against the negative impacts of tourism, not adding to when they're getting their biggest herd of visitors is likely to be a help.

Save that visit to Italy's Cinque Terre until autumn instead of joining the madding crowd when it's chock-a-block in the height of summer. Or forgo Iceland (see page 30), which has six international visitors for every resident, in favour of the Faroe Islands, an underpopulated archipelago that is part of Denmark. Typically, we're lured to a snowy Lapland between November and March for its Santa-related appeal – but head to Sweden or Finland in summer and you can enjoy long sunny days with bear watching and white water rafting and see the magical midnight sun. It's about thinking outside the brochure's typical fact box.

HOW TO
GET THERE

It's not merely about where we go or what we get up to while we're away – one of the most powerful ways to measure and mitigate impact is to consider how we get there and how we move around.

Go slow

Many of us have been enjoying slow holidays for years – we just didn't label them that. Ramblers would scoff at the idea of 'going slow' being a hot new trend. It's not only more eco-friendly to traverse new landscapes on foot, or by horse, bike or boat, but through positive slowness you get to savour the scenery as you pass it at eye level, feeling the fresh air on your face. Surrender to the flow and consider travel a form of meditation. As the founder of Responsible Travel, Justin Robertson, puts it:

"

Slow travel connects us to the soul of a place through its history, food, language and people.

"

What's the main thrust of slow travel? Skipping planes in favour of overland transport. In order to make this more feasible for time-poor individuals, work out whether you can escape for a longer stretch, or configure a way of working while you're on the road, to make it easier not to fly. When you are away, it's always a big eco win if you shirk domestic flights. Take things glacial. Plump for public transport, such as trains or electric buses. Once you're on the ground, it might even be better to explore on foot or by bike.

Green travel expert Richard Hammond advocates we make more of the slow travel journey. His website greentraveller.co.uk connects low-carbon transport to low-carbon holidays in the UK and Europe. Flying isn't as easy and cheap as it used to be, and as Hammond puts it, the journey by train and ferry can be fascinating, relaxing and fun; the adventure becomes part of the holiday. Also, in some ways, the slower you travel, the easier it is to be spontaneous. In the case of crossing France and Spain, for example, he suggests you have the flexibility to stop off en route in cities or unearth your own discoveries.

By train

Taking a train, not a plane, can cut emissions by up to 90 per cent, which is good to have in mind; but as Mark Smith, the Man in Seat 61 (a rail-planning website) says, it goes beyond this. 'The train journey becomes part of the holiday, a much nicer way to go – you may find you're doing yourself a favour, not just the planet. Booking trains can be more of a challenge than booking a flight, but – like most things in life – put in a little more effort and you may find you get a lot more out of it.' Since flying has become so much more accessible, young adventurers have started heading out to further-flung destinations, but when I was young, backpacking in your gap-year was synonymous with interrailing around Europe. We need to open our eyes again to what's right on our doorstep, and the environment will thank us too. Rail travel can be expensive but booking as far in advance as possible significantly cuts the cost.

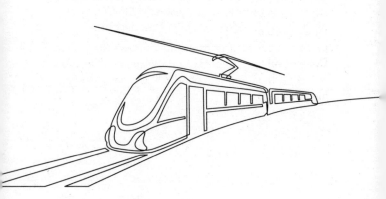

Again, Eurail passes can be quite pricey but Interrail has opened up with discounts for the under-27s. If you spend time online checking each country's own train service websites you may find you can patch together connections that work out cheaper.

Investigate accommodation well and you may find some hosts will have someone pick you up for free if you arrive by public transport, or they will reward you with cycle hire on the house, to make up for you not having your own wheels.

By road

Revving up the engine for a trip down Route 66, Jack Kerouac-style, isn't the greenest of images ... unless your road trip's four wheels are run by an electric motor. If you must drive to your destination, don't drive a gas-guzzler, pack it as lightly as possible, plan the most petrol-efficient route, keep those tyres properly pumped, your engine tuned, and drive at a good, steady pace. The reason it's important to look at the little details – such as matching the correct pressure – is that it can increase fuel economy by up to 3 per cent, which means lower emissions. (See **Daily travel** tips, page 23.) Caravans and motorhomes with virtually autonomous power supplies are in development, too.

By boat

An unhurried, more sustainable route to savour can be via the water. Think more on a scale of canal boat than mega-cruiseliner, or swapping in a ferry instead of a short-haul flight. Be creative when planning your circuit. If you're feeling especially dedicated to the cause, you could go further – research transits by cargo ship where you can rent a dinky cabin on a freighter ship and join their transit; as a guide, it takes about two weeks to get from Europe to North America.

By air

There's no point in looking sheepish: one of the best things you can do for the wellbeing of the planet is to decide not to fly. If you can't avoid planes completely, even just cutting down on unnecessary short-haul flights, and being more sensitive to the impact of the ones we do take, is a powerful positive. In Sweden, the antidote to *flygskam* – the flight-shaming movement – was *tågskryt* – train-bragging.

To many, electric airlines sound like a solution, but there's still a lot of debate around the safety, stability and number of charge cycles that their batteries can take before they need to be replaced. And it also requires us to investigate the ethics of mining the minerals needed to make these batteries and to verify the integrity of *those* supply chains ...

So, until they work out how to replace fossil fuels with household waste (*Back to the Future* flux-capacitor style), we can at least do our homework and make informed decisions about with whom we lift off. Generally, it's the taking off and landing part that spews out the most pollution, so it's good to fly direct, avoiding stopovers. And – sorry sybarites – economy-class-only planes *are* greener. Why? Because they get a lot more people from A to B, in a smaller space, using less fuel per head.

We are still awaiting full transparency from flight providers and there are some apps and platforms out there which help you navigate the options for lower-emission flying. If you're up to the challenge, you can do your own investigation into this. The factors that need considering are the aircraft, engine model and efficiency, that particular flight's load factor on the day of departure, seat configuration and food waste to differentiate. Carriers with lean-burn engines, smarter route technology and more sustainable fuel sources are worth looking for.

The recent paralysis of the world is undoubtedly going to mean changes in how all of us travel by air, temporarily if not permanently. Hopefully it's also allowed us all to reflect on how much we actually need to be flying – especially for business, now that we have seen how easily we can hold meetings online. So let us all take this opportunity to focus on travelling less and travelling better. Instead of hopping onto a low-cost flight for the sake of it, spend more time planning, prepping and looking forward to your dream getaway.

CYCLING HOLIDAYS

What's not to love about a mode of transport that lets you burn calories rather than fossil fuels?

The fact that this exercise is also going to help prolong your life expectancy is good for your own sustainability, if nothing else.

'It is by riding a bicycle that you learn the contours of a country best,' Ernest Hemingway famously said. But you may not want to familiarise yourself too deeply with the more dramatic ups and downs – which is a vote for cycling in the Low Countries, aka Benelux – Belgium, the Netherlands and Luxembourg. Whether you like it leisurely or in a low gear, France, Spain, Portugal and Italy all promise scenic countryside and coastal routes for differing degrees of exertion.

Until Oli Broom wheeled out his guided bike tours as The Slow Cyclist in 2014, this kind of holiday had generally been all about donning Lycra and pedalling as fast as you can – and that's not everyone's jam.

Definitely not mine. Cycling trips that are comfortable, relaxed, convivial experiences, where folks can be immersed in culture and get a much more authentic flavour of each particular corner of the world, thanks to sensitively thought-out itineraries and a clever way of bringing the right people together, have never been so appealing. Biking trips can be planned to suit your own fitness levels and desired pace; and best of all, you can always opt for electric-charged bikes. You can choose guided tours depending on your own interests.

WHERE TO STAY

When travelling, whether you're booking everything your-self or travelling with an operator, consider the following questions to ensure you're making good choices:

– Ask yourself: **'Where's my money going?'**

– Then research: **'Who will be benefitting from my traveller cash?'**

– Ask your agent or operator: **'Does everyone involved in this itinerary receive a living wage?'**

– Ask hotels questions such as: **'How much of your power comes from renewable energy sources?'** and **'How is your waste processed?'**

It seems that googling 'hotel in [insert name of chosen destination]' is still the favoured way to research favour-ites – but I'm hopeful that we'll soon be searching for the likes of 'zero-waste hotel in [insert name of chosen destination]'.

Looking for
eco accommodation

A good starting point when assessing how green accommodation is, is looking at how that property was constructed or whether they have seals that denote sustainable credentials, and how they've been built. EarthCheck is a leading system of scientific benchmarking, certification and advice, as is Travelife; BREEAM (Building Research Establishment Environmental Assessment Method) and LEED (Leadership in Energy and Environmental Design) denote green building principles. The WELL Building Standard takes a holistic approach to health-addressing behaviour, operations and design, with a performance-based system for measuring and certifying the wellbeing of built environments.

'Slow aesthetics' is a design philosophy where buildings, furniture and objects are made of natural materials, such as wood, natural stone and warm metals. As these materials age, there's also a deepening of patina and charm. In this way, objects have a longer life and don't need updating, so demonstrate a sensitive approach to design that is conscious about resources. *Cradle to Cradle: Remaking the Way We Make Things* by William McDonough and Michael Braungart is what led to the creation of the term 'cradle to cradle', which is associated with the Slow Design movement, and denotes waste-free production systems.

ACCESSIBILITY AND INCLUSIVITY

Green travel isn't merely about treading more lightly on this planet of ours; it's about improving the quality of life for all its people.

Sustainable stays should also fling open their doors to all travellers regardless of age, gender, sexuality and ideology. They should prioritise diversity in terms of who they hire and who they speak to in their marketing. Accessibility and inclusivity are oft-overlooked key considerations within sustainable travel — we all deserve equal access to the same full experiences. It's about much more than wheelchair ramps; those living with compromise want to feel comfortable and confident on trips. A quarter of all humans live with a disability; even if that doesn't include you or your travel companions, helping amplify the conversation around inclusivity and accessibility is one way of being a kinder traveller. In the UK, the Good Access Guide and the Blue Badge Access Awards celebrate venues that welcome everyone through their doors whatever their needs or physical challenges.

Inclu Travel's Richard Thompson matches itineraries to travellers' desires and requirements. Obviously, some destinations are more limited than others for those with accessibility needs – wheelchair-adapted taxis being one of the greatest barriers – but Thompson grills travellers and suppliers about everything from what assistance is available at the airports to homing in on hotels with hoists for beds and the bath. Most services and facilities are born not from empathy or inclusivity but from legislative requirements. 'Slowly there's increased awareness – but it could still be much, much better and accessible travel could be much more accessible.' The travel disruptor's first question to travellers? Not 'What's your disability?' but 'Where do you dream of going?'

It's so important to see the world through as wide range of perspectives as possible. I love following @nomadnesstribe and @theblacktravelalliance who remind all that we need to hear more travel stories from people of colour. Disability activist @sophlmorg shows us how to be a wheelchair adventurer and @TraveleyesLtd is a must follow for visually impaired and blind travellers. Kareemah Ashiru of @hijabi-globetrotter is a go-to for muslim-friendly travel tips and @fatgirlstravelling boosts Fat Activism through a travel lens.

Camping

Camping might have always seemed an environmentally friendly kind of holiday, but some sites are going to be greener than others. Who doesn't love the idea of a light touch and low impact on the land? If you've been spoiled by a diet of hotel-based holidays, a common-or-garden tent may not appeal, but experiencing the countryside can now also be enjoyed by bunking up in the new generation of aesthetically-pleasing glamping lodges, mega-tents or beautifully-styled tipis or trailers.

Things have moved on a lot since mealtimes meant heating baked beans on a trangia, thanks to glamping aficionados such as Canopy & Stars, who have curated a selection of more stylish canvas abodes complete with fluffy pillows. Camp meals can now include the best fresh-from-the-farm grazing and craft beers. Over in France, 'camping écologique' has popularised partly tented cabins or there being an organic eatery.

"

As ever, when it comes to what you take with you, less is more, and you can follow the usual edict of quality over quantity.

"

If you don't have your own tent already, consider investing in a long-lasting one if you think you will use it again and again. You can buy cheap nylon pop-ups for next-to-nothing these days (as favoured by the one-use-only festival set) but you are likely going to need to replace it after only a few uses – better to invest in something that has a longer life, obviously. Alternatively, you could try to borrow one from a friend or seek out a professional tent-rental service. For a more luxe camping getaway, there are companies that will put up a rented bell tent or yurt for you, often including inflatable airbeds and fresh bed linen.

As we all know, good-quality sleep is important, especially on a holiday, so when buying sleeping bags and airbeds, your best bet is to ask in a specialist shop which of the latest products are more eco and why. Quiz them about which wind-up or solar-powered torches, radios and phone chargers are best, too, as these ranges are ever advancing. As usual, it is best not to go for the cheapest option that won't last. In general, look for products made with end-of-life materials or from responsible manufacturers, and don't use anything that has a short shelf life and can't be reused or recycled, such as disposable barbecues. Travel towels can look and feel a little pathetic, but they are both lightweight and super absorbent. If you're going really wild, water may not be on tap, so stock up with big refillable bottles rather than reaching for the bottled stuff in supermarkets.

There was a time when hospitality – the respect and honour shown from host to guest – was prized as one of the most important of virtues.

Hotels and lodges

There was a time when hospitality – the respect and honour shown from host to guest – was prized as one of the most important of virtues.

A vital part of the travel-prepping stage is discerning which hosts not only talk a good sustainability game but are actually doing it. The hotel business has changed dramatically in recent times, to be less about kindness and more about property assets, management contracts, revenue and profit margins. At a time when our Instagram feeds are teeming with plastic-entangled turtles and motivational quotes reminding us to kick our planet-bashing habits, it's important to be alert about the hotel you're booking into.

Now that everyone is throwing around words such as 'eco-friendly', it's critical to have your antenna tuned to picking up on 'greenwash'. It helps to know how to distinguish between tokenism and real activism to ensure you aren't seduced by a false green sheen.

WHAT TO LOOK FOR

- **Is there a section on the website dedicated to sustainability creds and corporate social responsibility (CSR)?** Can you spot reputable accreditation logos? Does the hotel support charities, community or sustainability initiatives?

- **Energy:** are they clear on their efficiency in terms of their use of renewables, lighting, heating systems?

- **Water:** do they mention low-flow showers, low-consumption toilets or recycling greywater or rainwater harvesting?

- **Waste:** do they follow the 'reduce, reuse, recycle' principle for glass, paper, card, plastic and metal? Do they compost?

- **Employment:** what percentage of the team is hired from the immediate community? Do they invest in training? Do they even talk about their social impact?

- **Getting around:** do they encourage guests to use public transport, offer cycles or walking tips?

- **Food and drink:** is it all sourced locally or, even better, grown on site? Do they favour organic? Do they have a no beef or no imported branded drinks policy?

- **Housekeeping:** can you reuse towels and sheets to save laundering?

- **Gardens and greenery:** do they make a point of confirming their gardens are biodiverse or planted with native flora? Do they skip displaying cut flowers in favour of plants?

- **Culture and conservation:** is their mention of caring about supporting indigenous crafts and artisans done in a meaningful way? Do they support rewilding or land preservation projects?

Bringing their back-of-house activity to the front of your mind is a good rule of thumb. The hotel's operations, housekeeping and engineering practices are increasingly as important to guests as the comforts and facilities facing them. Rather than crowd-pleasers spilling over with disposable amenities, we should be digging deeper and saluting hotels or campsites – chains or independents – with dazzling performance indicators and ambitious energy-reduction targets.

Book rooms at a big international chain hotel and it may be an address that marries a wealthy overseas asset-owner with the management of a well-oiled hospitality mega-machine. The mechanics of their loyalty programme and staff training may make you feel a sense of belonging, but chances are you probably aren't doing much for that farming community you passed as you turned into the driveway.

A general reduction in free amenities (think hotel-room toiletries) is best, otherwise we just use all that junk simply because it's there. Then we can't resist squirrelling it away in our bags to take home, knowing that they will replenish it. Beware cutesy pseudo-eco stuff – presenting a disposable razor wrapped in hemp twine or a panda-poo-paper box does not make it sustainable. In fact, the packaging only adds to the junk destined for landfill. We need to beat our addiction to things and convenience and rewire our perception of luxury and value. I'm all for being surprised and delighted, but it won't be landfill-fodder that sparks joy on my travels; it will be that spirit-lifting feeling that I'm leaving less in my wake.

ENERGY-EFFICIENT OR NET-ZERO HOTELS

While you're on the road, you can lessen your carbon load by supporting energy-efficient hotels, eating locally and seasonally and avoiding beef at mealtimes. When staying in remote areas, just visualise what's required to fly in all their supplies. It's natural that plant-based organic diets have a lower 'foodprint' – the nickname for the ecological impact of the food industry, from production to wastage. Self-sufficient hosts who harness the power of solar energy are doing more. Some businesses aim to achieve 'net-zero', where they've measured all the emissions released by their activity and balanced it out through offsetting or by buying carbon credits. (Carbon offsetting is the idea that the negative emissions from one activity can be cancelled out by the purchase of credits towards the investment in schemes elsewhere. There is much debate around carbon trading as all schemes are not equal. It's best to reduce the carbon emissions in the first place.) The smallest adjustments on our part can also make a big difference: turn that air-conditioning from a cool 19°C (66°F) to a slightly warmer 22°C (71°F), and you'll be shaving 10 per cent off the energy consumption.

FOGO ISLAND INN, CANADA

*This place was a gamechanger for me
– a design hotel on a tiny, far-flung
rugged isle, just south of Greenland.*

Northeast Newfoundland isn't the obvious spot for a dream escape, but ever since I'd heard Zita Cobb speak about why she built this inn on the island where she grew up, I'd wanted to go.

Born the sixth of seven children to an illiterate fisherman, Zita Cobb eventually retired from a high-powered role in finance as the wealthiest woman in Canada. Having watched the economy of her birthplace evaporate through drastic fishing restrictions, she decided to create a business that would reinvigorate the entire community. First came the arts-supporting Shorefast Foundation, with its angular artist studios perched on the rocks. Unemployed boat builders were redeployed as furniture makers and local craftspeople transferred their quilt-making skills to creating items to be sold in the hotel shop. Zita celebrated their normal in a way that had an exotic allure for jaded luxury travellers. Fogo is a hotel with a conscience that proves this isn't about creating a charity model but creating an economic engine.

In a clever concept mimicking food nutrition labelling, the Shorefast Foundation originated and developed the idea of the Economic Nutrition certification mark, which has the same power to have a positive impact on buying choices as nutritional breakdowns do on our food. It promotes awareness and transparency around business practices, geographical provenance of goods and sustainability. At Fogo, labour is the most significant investment; all payment stays in the same geo-coordinates; not a penny is squandered on advertising. Really, we need Zita's Economic Nutrition labelling on everything, so we can always choose the healthiest option. At Fogo, Cobb has essentially created a blueprint for a new model of luxury hospitality.

Economic Nutrition^{CM} — **fogo island inn**

NIGHTLY STAY (ACTUAL 2018)	WHERE THE MONEY GOES
Labour	**49%**
Food, Room Supplies	**12%**
Commissions, Fees	**5%**
Operations, Admin	**18%**
Sales, Marketing	**4%**
Surplus (Reinvested in the community of Fogo Island)	**12%**

Economic Benefit Distribution:

Fogo Island	65%	Canada	19%
Newfoundland	13%	Rest of the world	3%

Economic Nutrition is a certification trademark of Shorefast Foundation, used under license by Shorefast Social Enterprises Inc.

Volunteering holidays

The concept of voluntourism sparks debate, as some opportunist travel planners have come up with seemingly do-gooding holidays, but when you analyse these they have the potential to do much more harm than good. Volunteering holidays in underprivileged destinations shouldn't just mean a gratifying time for the visitors, and a chance to share some virtue-signalling shots on social – it needs to be change-making for the communities you're visiting or for their conservation. That's not to say there aren't loads of schemes out there which are genuine forces for good, just do your research beforehand.

"

The dream scenario is that you book a trip that is ethical and not exploitative, and you being somewhere is genuinely of help to the local communities, with no one profiting from your time away.

"

Working holidays hosted by conservation charities, such as the National Trust, invite participants to contribute to citizen science projects while getting close to nature. During Barter Week in November, owners of B&Bs around the world trade free accommodation for goods or services, such as carpentry or IT skills. After the bushfires,

Australia revised visa restrictions to allow those planning a working holiday to be able to volunteer in the worst-hit regions as a way of applying for extended visas.

Another great example is The Leap in Southern Namibia, which has been inviting clients to help to save the endangered rhinos by creating a safe haven for the endangered species and through educating the next generation on conservation. Over the years, The Leap has sent groups to remove fences, chop down poisonous vegetation, build dams and set up watering holes.

Blue Ventures is another initiative that hosts expeditions which are part of a carefully considered transformative approach for catalysing and sustaining locally led marine conservation. They work in places where the ocean is vital to local cultures and economies and are committed to protecting marine biodiversity in ways that benefit coastal people.

HOW TO BOOK

Looking at your supply chain and where your spending settles is one of the most important things that a consumer can do.

Hopefully this doesn't make you sigh, because it does sound a tad dull and technical. It just means ensuring that every time you pay someone for an aspect of your travel you are aiming to hand it over to a good business, that does good. It can be fun figuring out who the good guys are. Having a positive economic impact is such an important way of being greener and making our travels count.

When it comes to the actual clicking-to-book stage, think about buying directly from independent providers, just like you would purchase goods straight from a maker or supplier rather than going to Amazon. You might book through a sharing-economy platform and think it's sustainable, but it might mostly be benefitting the techpreneurs creaming off the commission. It's simple – it's about choosing suppliers and services where stakeholders are considered above shareholders and purpose is prized over maximising profit. And ensuring as much stays in local bank accounts as possible.

Who to trust

Transparency is everything. The way a company communicates how they are contributing to the greater good is important. You don't want them to be overstating what they're doing, especially if their supposedly eco actions are really just aimed at saving their business money. The real heroes of hospitality reward their customers for minimising their carbon footprint; for example, a hotel that incentivises you to skip housekeeping services for a couple of days in return for a cocktail on the house.

There are few universally recognised standard metrics or certifications; ESG (Environmental, Social, Governance) metrics can be inaccurate because they can be qualitatively manipulated. We are all familiar with the green yin-and-yang-like Fairtrade seal, there are no simple equivalent symbols or standardised stamps to represent broader social or environmental impact – on a national or global level. If a business is B Corp-certified, you know it meets the highest standards of verified social and environmental performance, public transparency and legal accountability. Accreditations from third-party assessments can signify an operator has conformed to a standard of practice. Specifically in travel, EarthCheck is a reliable marque (see certifications, page 127).

Seeking out social enterprises

An inspiring way to plan an itinerary is by plotting stops along the way to visit businesses that aim to promote positive social change. Tour operators that empower local communities through ensuring that as many links in their trips' supply chains have a conscience are the ones to favour; this includes the likes of G Adventures, Steppes, Intrepid Travel, Up Norway, Responsible Travel and Wild Frontiers.

A social enterprise is a business which works with local communities and tends to mean much more meaningful interactions through engaging you with the culture in a more immersive way, or by allowing you to understand the challenges facing that destination, and contribute to a way of helping.

The founder of G Adventures, Bruce Poon Tip, has launched scores of social enterprises over the years, which tackle poverty, create jobs and launch responsible tourism from Peru to Vietnam. 'We have always measured our success as a business through local benefit and positive impact,' he says. 'Tourism is one of the main ways by which we can redistribute wealth to countries that need it, and one of the main ways we help change the perception of a place.' Their projects with their non-profit partner Plane-terra have different focuses. By including visits to projects that also educate travellers about little-known issues, our travels can help encourage better equality in society.

Ethical insurance

Hold on to your hat – there are insurance companies out there who care for people and the planet, not just profit. Do your homework around underwriters. What you need to look for is whether they have an ethical policy on investments. You could consult UnfriendCoal.com – this coalition of NGOs calls out the heroes and zeroes in this sector. As with anything, you're going to want to be giving your cash to companies that are transparent around their investments. Consider supporting companies that prioritise the greater good and contribute to their tax system.

66

This sector is evolving fast, and if you spend a little time researching you should get a good sense of who walks their talk.

99

The Good Shopping Guide has an Ethical Company Index, which considers the impact on the environment, animals, people from policy providers.

CAFÉ WITH A CAUSE

When I went to see the Taj Mahal in Agra, it wasn't the Mughal majesty of the marble that blew me away, it was pausing at **Sheroes Hangout** nearby, a café set up by an Indian journalist to support victims of acid attacks. Women survivors welcomed us in for tea and told us their tales, which weren't just heart-wrenching but also heart-warming. Thanks to this roadside caff, they've been able to move beyond the stigma and have been given a new lease of life. Patrons are asked to pay a donation for items chosen from their menu of drinks or snacks to support their cause. Our hosts' witty observations about the world made us laugh as we enjoyed our cuppas and, before we left, many had connected with us on social media, where I continue to see endless comments from their adoring fans and friends from around the world.

- Walking tours hosted by those who've faced challenges is a poignant way of getting under the skin of that place and learn about it in a new light. In the UK, **Invisible Cities** trains those who have experienced homelessness to become walking tour guides. In India, **Salaam Baalak Trust City Walk** was funded by Mira Nair's 1988 film *Salaam Bombay!* to help street kids have a safe place to sleep and access to schooling.

- **Small Projects Istanbul** is a community space where Syrian refugee women in Turkey access language, computer and leadership lessons as well as coaching in crafts such as sewing, silk-screening and jewellery design. With the support of Intrepid Travel, SPI hosts a fashion-focused social enterprise, Muhra. Their Urban Adventures In Focus Tour: The Olive Tree of Istanbul and Turkey: Women's Expedition invites travellers there to enjoy a Syrian meal with the volunteers.

- In Jerusalem, the Dom, or Domba, face regular discrimination due to these traditionally nomadic people not being fully integrated into either Israeli or Palestinian societies. By visiting the **Domari Community Centre**, you don't only get a cultural and craft experience, but buying their handicrafts helps support the women and children of this community in many ways.

- In Greece, high unemployment among the young has resulted in homelessness being a serious issue. **Shedia Home** in Athens is a non-profit café-bar-restaurant that employs those experiencing social exclusion. Pause here for a coffee break and educational talks from your guide and help support an important cause.

Carbon offsetting and tree planting

Global warming relates to the volume of greenhouse gases released that is creating a layer in the atmosphere like a planet-swaddling blanket. Our footprint is the total amount of greenhouse gases – the emissions – produced by us, or a business, usually represented in tonnes of carbon dioxide. One offsetting credit or unit usually represents a tonne of carbon avoided, sequestered or captured on your behalf.

When you calculate emissions to be offset – each tonne of CO_2 to be countered – it tends to be pegged on buying emission reductions made in another location. But not all offsetting schemes are created equal. A Gold Standard seal is given to the most credible offset programmes, with the highest levels of assurance that outcomes have been achieved with certifiable impacts on UN Sustainable Development Goals (SDGs), from water benefits to renewable energy certificates to health or gender equality benefits. A Verified Carbon Standard (VCS) status denotes full transparency and public trackability. It's the nitty-gritty that matters: you want to look for credentials validated by the International Carbon Reduction and Offset Alliance (ICROA). Their support also helps with other SDGs, such as communities, wildlife and incomes in deprived areas. Most importantly, their projects are permanent (before becoming accountable, tree-planters of yore could take your cash but then grow timber for questionable for-profit projects).

Planting trees is a wonderful thing to counter carbon, but shouldn't be considered an easy offsetting fix.

To truly absorb carbon from the atmosphere and fix it in the soil can take a tree a lifetime. Much is re-emitted into the atmosphere at night or fixed into the bark and leaves, returning to the atmosphere as soon as the tree is cut or burned. When it dies and biodegrades, this produces methane, which has a greenhouse effect 30 times stronger than carbon dioxide. Is your mind boggling yet? That's why it is better to focus on reducing emissions.

TreeSisters is a charity that facilitates female tree-planting projects in deforested tropical areas. It's important to consider what trees are planted where, for the maximum sequestering of carbon from the air – and it's all the better when there is a socio-economic benefit.

One of the best ways to tackle climate change, as acknowledged by the United Nations, is to invest in the lives of women in remote rural areas: this improves education, means they get married later in life, and have fewer children. As the ever-spiralling-out-of-control global population is one of the most significant contributors to all the ecological factors exaggerating climate change, this is significant. Knowledge is power.

Responsible Travel launched Green Flying Duty as an alternative to offsetting. 'Until we do have solutions in place to fly clean and green,' says CEO Justin Francis, 'we have put a duty onto flying – all the money raised through this will be ring-fenced for accelerating progress for research and development and to improve rail networks to bring the future forward.'

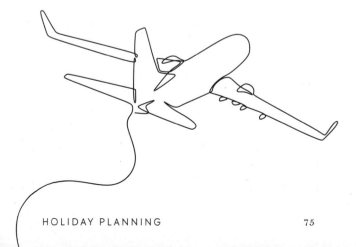

TIPS FOR DIFFERENT TYPES OF TRIPS

SOLO

If you're heading off on an adventure on your own, it makes sense to plan further in advance to ensure there's availability where you want to stay. Factor in some volunteering as a great way of contributing positively and meeting others (check out the section on responsible volunteering on page 115). Bear in mind the culture of where you want to go and whether as a single girl/guy that might affect the dynamic between you and the locals. For visiting religious landmarks, as with all travel, you'll want long sleeves, skirts or trousers, so always pack culturally appropriate attire – but when you're an independent traveller, it's even more important to be sensitive to cultural sensitivities. Don't default to taxis, instead favour public transport or walking — it can be even more enjoyable when you're solo. Seeking out hostel or dorm-style accommodation isn't just a great way of meeting others in the common spaces, it costs less and you'll be responsible for using a lot fewer utilities than if you were in a big suite or apartment for one.

FAMILY

For hassle- and headache-free holidays, it can be best to keep it simple. There's never been a better time to staycation or swap extravagant exotic escapes for comfortable camping.

"

> Holidays are a valuable time to engage young 'uns with nature and culture, but in a relaxed way.

"

Ditch digital devices and walk, hike, bike, swim, beach comb. Pack old-fashioned books and colouring pencils so kids can draw what they see. Create treasure hunts with tick-lists of what to look out for. Imagination and creativity is what distinguishes us humans from robots, so let's keep it fuelled. Activate budding activists and empower them as citizen scientists. Download the Plastic Patrol app, head off on a bit of litter-picking and record and contribute data for this environmental initiative. Getting the public involved in valuable field research is a great way to help conservation projects, as data collection can be the most time-consuming part. Surfers Against Sewage is a campaign group that rallies their community to clear our oceans, and the group asks surfers to report on water conditions and take action where needed.

If you're planning a long-haul trip, get everyone involved in the process and weigh up where to go and why. If your kids are old enough, discuss what issues matter most to them and choose a trip that aligns with their passions – reconnecting with nature, supporting wildlife conservation, empowering women or tracing historical, scientific or geographical interests. Most kids love animals, but zoos and aquariums are rarely dream inhabitants for their inmates – unless they're a non-profit promoting conservation and education. Do a little background research. Opting for fantastical accommodation such as eco-cabins, yurts or treehouses will also help ensure the kids feel immersed in somewhere exciting.

Golden rules on the go: don't clamber over cultural sites or take anything away, always avoid using anything disposable and minimise waste. Connect with local cultures – try new foods rather than sticking to favourites from home which need to be imported. It can be easier to defer to plain pasta preferences, but rewarding finicky little ones for trying entry-level rice dishes or make sampling new fruits or vegetables is an adventure in itself and they may thank you later in life. Picky-eating teens may be coaxed into trying more exotic flavours if you cultivate curiosity and model behaviour when it comes to showing willing and an open mind.

ROMANTIC

The most heart-stirring, honeymoon-worthy places are often naturally eco ... Imagine that off-grid island where your treehouse built from driftwood is ensconced in an unfettered wilderness. Just-plucked or -caught ingredients are served to you outdoors, where you have your feet in the sand under the stars. Eco and aphrodisiacal. Technology is a wonderful thing, but as personal devices and wifi connect us, romance can often allude us. Switch off your smartphone and talk to those you meet along the way, instead of staying plugged into folks back home. Learn about the culture you're in by genuinely experiencing it. Because of the energy required to keep servers running, cloud storage gives aviation a run for its money in greenhouse gas emissions. Using your phone for all that phototaking and sharing has a carbon footprint of its own. The less downloading and charging you do, the greener you are being. Or forgo that tried-and-tested, far-flung beach resort and invest in somewhere special that is much closer to home, that you'd never usually find an excuse to splash out on. You might not be guaranteed the tropical beaches, but a spell in a grand hotel in Scotland with an incredible spa or elegant country-house estate with a Michelin-starred chef might be as rewarding and free of the hassles and impact of international escapades.

4

BUSINESS

Ask first: do you need to fly there for that meeting, or might video-conferencing do? As the spring of 2020 swiftly showed us, we can get quality face time through our computers. Sometimes Zooming won't cut it, though, so if you need to go on a business trip or attend a trade show, at least make the most of it. Schedule a 'workcation' – blending your work time with your holiday time – so you don't do a long-haul there and back only to fly over the same landmass again soon after. While it's easy to hop into a cab, especially if you're expensing it, consider car-sharing with a colleague or opt for public transport – it can be more pleasant than sitting in solid traffic. And, of course, try to stay in eco-friendly hotels. If your corporate travel team is a slave to loyalty programmes, at least talk to them about identifying the greenest options. The more people who raise the topic, the more companies can effect change. An increasing number of companies are scrutinising their corporate social responsibility policies so they're better accountable, as well as their environmental, social and governance criteria so they cannot just be seen as being aware of the impact of all their actions, but allow for their impact to be more measurable.

WELLNESS

Since being greener is essentially about wellbeing for the world, let's think deeper about time spent in spas. I have found it strange that when it comes to wellbeing there's such a disconnect between concern for our own health and that of the planet as a whole. My problem with some retreats is that it's just not relaxing to see so much treated water and energy expended to enhance the experience for its visitors – often at the cost of locals. We know how much plastic ends up contaminating the oceans, yet spas are spilling over with pre-packaged, single-use, disposable undies and the like. The spa industry turns over trillions – the sector needs to up its game to make its business a more potent force for good.

Choose hosts who invest in water-saving tricks, such as low-flow showers and watering their gardens with grey-water. Look for the places that use all-natural therapies enhanced with fruit, veg and spices. Sometimes, you just can't improve on nature at its most raw.

Rather than being lavished with huge fluffy white towels and leaving a knot-in-stomach-inducing wake of things to be washed and dried, there's nothing wrong with turning down many a robe or disposable slipper. Say to staff that you won't take the dressing gown and check it's ok to use your own flip-flops. That way you spare landfills and laundry, and might spur them to think about how some customers might be more sensitive to what we leave in our wake.

WHAT TO PACK

What to take or not take? Let's consider three of the sustainability 'R's. Firstly, do a **reduce** evaluation. How much do we really need to take with us? Can we survive on supplies we already have? Then look through the **recycle** and the **reuse** lenses. Choose a good brand if you've got to make a purchase. A sustainable buy could be made from eco-friendly, chemical-free materials or is going to last the long-haul and won't need replacing.

LUGGAGE

Let's examine the anatomy of your suitcase or bag. How's it made? What's it made with? Will it last ages? Is it light? You want to find the sweet spot – every kilo counts. Many luggage brands make various claims, but decide on what you like and use logic: a good guide is that it's rarely the cheapest option that's best if you want something that will last or that was made in a factory where people were paid properly. Obviously, any attempts to bring down the volume of your packing is great – and carry-on luggage is the holy grail.

CLOTHING

We're brainwashed into thinking that our escapes need to be dripping with fun fast-fashion and cheap-chic accessories. Think: can you persevere with what you already have? Probably. If you must have something new, charity shops are a great way to pick up second-hand steals, especially when they take a curated, cherry-picked approach to donations – whether it's sweaters for ski trips or recent-season sundresses for posher summer forays. Or try clothing rental companies where you pay a fee that is a fraction of the price tag to borrow fancy threads for a week at a time. We should be trying to cut down on the amount of clothes we pack, but washing while away from home is a drag and sending a few items to be dry-cleaned in a big chain hotel can be very expensive. Luckily there are some great options for travel wash that you can pack to take with you.

66

Think: can you persevere with what you already have? Probably.

99

ETHICAL ACCESSORIES

Really need brand new? Pick a purveyor whose creations are the lovechild of a good cause and great design. Buy a pair of Pala Eyewear's stylish sunglasses and you are helping them set up long-term eye-care solutions in Africa, including eye tests and the provision of specs for people to access education or employment. There are more and more sustainable fashion brands around now that have a secondary social purpose. Just don't be hoodwinked by the high-street fast-fashion brands with their pseudo eco collections — try to choose independent brands set up with the sole intention of social impact over selling quantity over quality.

TOILETRIES

Those dinky little filled toiletries that are small enough to take in your carry-on are tempting but are a nightmare from a single-use-plastic point of view. Instead, invest in a few refillable bottles that come under the 100ml mark and simply fill up from what you already have at home. Better still, look for solid shampoo and cleanser bars which often come with reusable packaging so you can simply stick them in your washbag and you're all set. Show some love for skincare that is ethical, biodegradable and free from chemical nasties. Understandably, there has been an upsurge in the use of disinfectant chemicals in recent times, but the fact is, killing all bacteria unilaterally is bad for our health and the planet's. It's worth considering eco-friendly, naturally clean environments as an antidote to immune systems becoming even more vulnerable and compromised.

We need
to beat our
addiction to
things and
convenience
and rewire our
perception
of luxury and
value.

EATING AND DRINKING ACCOUTREMENTS

Eating and drinking on the go can be a very easy way to generate unnecessary waste. Now that more and more airports and travel stops have free water dispensers, keep clutching that BPA-free drinking-water bottle, especially if it's made from captured ocean plastics. For when it's not filtered: take a LifeStraw, personal purification for safe-to-drink water, wherever you are. Just think about all those overpriced plastic-wrapped sandwiches and sugary snacks we buy on the hoof just because we didn't do a little pre-planning. My fave lunchbox alternative is a stainless-steel leakproof box which feels more hipster than housewife. Put together your own 'zero-waste travel kit' – mine is a refillable coffee cup, a metal straw and a bamboo cutlery set – which means no need for any disposables when you pick up food along the way.

AND WHAT NOT TO PACK ...

Anything single-use is a no-no: Wet Wipes (what's wrong with an old-fashioned fabric flannel?) through to disposable feminine hygiene products. (Attention those of you who menstruate: just think of all those tampons clogging sanitation systems and landfills. Try a menstrual cup, you could save thousands of disposable products over your lifetime.) Anything bulky that you might not actually need — sure, take those heavy-duty hiking boots, but only if you're actually going to wear them. Then when you have all your chattels stacked by the front door ready to go, recall these words from Coco Chanel: 'Before you leave the house, look in the mirror and take one thing off.' Except apply this to all that you've packed ... And chances are you don't need to take all that stuff. Making like a minimalist isn't just channelling the world's most elegant woman, it's a hallmark of being more eco.

'ARE YOU CARRYING ANYTHING FOR SOMEONE ELSE?'

Well, yes, actually – you could be. Pack for a Purpose remind us that travellers can help do their bit by finding out who needs what, and where. Hotels can play a role in connecting supplies to those in need. Taking along some essentials that are helpful to the less fortunate wherever you're heading is a great plan. Since 2010, travellers have taken nearly 200,000 kilos of supplies – from books to toothbrushes – to more than 60 countries thanks to the Pack for a Purpose website listing hotels in destinations where need is great.

WHILE
YOU'RE AWAY

CHAPTER 2

Most human activity tends to have a negative impact on the world in some way. Truth is, whatever we do, we're more likely to be depleting natural resources than replenishing them. But with careful thought and a bit of research, you can find lots of ways to make your trips a force for good. As Paulo Coelho says, there is always a gap between intention and action. Let's close that gap by understanding what to look out for and what we can do.

Being woke is not enough – we all need to be better at walking our talk. Yes, social media has been powerful at amplifying voices and disseminating messages, but it has also meant a rise in armchair activists, who – instead of actually effecting change through their behaviour – think that by retweeting motivational ditties or by advocating reform through their Insta feed, they're doing their bit. Better to boycott unethical businesses and travel services or to lobby policymakers to get change rolling. Understand and do something positive to tackle the causes of the world's problems, don't just shout about the symptoms. And before you leave home, consider how best to minimise and shut down all your utilities so you don't end up using two household's worth of energy while you're on holiday. Simple things like ensuring all lights are switched off, any devices that don't need to be left on (your fridge, for example) are unplugged and, depending on the time of year, switch off your heating. (The exception to this is during a cold winter when you're in danger of flooding from frozen pipes, so make sure to check the weather forecast before you do this.)

KEEP IT
LOCAL

Leaving a place better than we found it is a good guide to gallivanting. Stick to this mantra as much as you can and you're more than halfway to being greener.

Typically, for every $100 spent by a tourist from a developed country in a developing country, only $5 stays in the local economy (according to the United Nations, 2016), so leaving money with those most in need is another winner. Especially when you can pay those most in need cash in hand for their services.

So how do you go about making sure that the money you spend stays local? The best way to do this is always think 'small and local'; visit markets instead of supermarkets, book guesthouses directly rather than through international chains. Buy eco-friendly indigenous crafts where you're paying the maker or artisan directly. You won't just be helping that native producer hawking their delicious small-batch baked goods or that humble B&B host, chances are whatever you buy will taste/experience/feel more authentic, too.

Holidays that consider the wellbeing of people in a less well-off destination, and which prioritise involving locals in decision-making, have a direct positive, social and economic impact. It's not always easy to find out this information yourself, so look for companies that can do some of this work for you. G Adventures has for many years hosted tours which aim to leave as much money as possible in local economies, through hotels, transport, restaurants, experiences and guides. Their Ripple Score audits hundreds of trips and evaluates every supplier for local ownership. Countless trips on the website now have an out-of-100 score (with 100 being the most spent locally), which allows transparency on how much spent in a destination goes directly into the hands of locals. The average score on their site is 93.

GETTING AROUND

How we get from A to B whether in
our daily lives or when we travel,
is seriously significant.

By foot

The simplest tip: walk, walk, walk. Clearly, the lowest-carbon way to get anywhere is on your own two feet. It's free and good exercise and it's a brilliant way to get to know the place you're visiting and discover hidden gems.

By bus, tram or subway

Don't take taxis, tackle local public transport instead –
it's the best way to get to know a place and its nuances.
Metros and subway trains tend to produce 80 per cent
lower emissions than single-occupancy vehicles. Yes,
hopping into a car might seem easier, but public transport
is usually a winner. Hong Kong leads the way, with Seoul
and Singapore among the other Asian cities topping the
Sustainable Cities Mobility Index for transport. In Europe,
Zürich, Frankfurt, Paris, Prague and Vienna are among
those best served. Tips on how best to tackle public trans-
portation will vary for each destination. Before you set off,
get advice from a reliable local on how and where to pay
your fare, or if there are some great passes especially for
visitors or which routes to avoid or prioritise.

By bike

Firstly, there's the boon of no environmental impact from
getting around, and secondly, hubs with good cycle provision tend to have better air quality, too. But the appeal of
different destinations according to their cycling schemes
will also vary depending on your proficiency and who
you're travelling with. Tourist information centres will be
able to guide you how to hire bikes or scooters and whether there are trails suited to parents hoping to head out
with tag-alongs, pods and trailers. Places with the best
public bike-share schemes include Copenhagen and the
Netherlands, which also have plenty of appealing cycle
paths for less-confident riders.

THE 5 'R'S

As modern tourists, travelling in a responsible, green way may look very similar to the practices you use at home to reduce your impact. Keep in mind the five 'R's of sustainability:

REFUSE

REDUCE

REUSE

RECYCLE

ROT

- **Say no to anything disposable.** Arm yourself with Tupperware, lidded boxes and reusable water bottles to avoid the need for any single-use containers.

- **Reduce emissions** by using public transport whenever possible and spare your reliance on all resources through quick showers, judicious laundering and not using towels or changing bedsheets unnecessarily.

- **Pre-prep picnics** – don't buy packaged 'on-the-go' or ready-made food. When staying in self-catering cottages or camping, use the best of what is available locally to make simple, delicious meals. Cook from scratch using recipes that don't involve imported exotic ingredients.

- **Insist on local and seasonal**, favouring small independent producers (low food miles guaranteed). When travelling, make sure you hit farmers' markets, family-run butchers, greengrocers and bakeries.

- **Make do and mend.** Rather than buying new, darn worn socks and sew loose buttons back on, even on holiday.

- **When you eat out, only order what you think you can actually eat there and then,** otherwise check first that the kitchen composts leftovers, or does doggy bags.

The very
essence of
what green
travel is all
about is
the need
to conserve
natural
resources.

MINIMISE YOUR IMPACT

So you've done the work in making sure your decisions about where to go and how to travel there were as positive as possible. Now we need to continue that good work when we're actually away.

Cut down on your energy and water use

The very essence of what green travel is all about is the need to conserve natural resources. I'd be willing to bet that most travellers, whether they care about sustainability or not, would confess to using more energy while they're away than they would typically use at home. Why? Maybe it's because someone else is paying the bill, or maybe it's because they don't want to have to think about anything too deeply on vacation. In hotels, thanks to electronic key cards, we are now spared the hassle of having to remember to turn each and every thing off ourselves, manually. But it's worth remembering to do that if you find yourself staying somewhere more low-fi, or in self-catering accommodation. Check the lights and air-conditioning in particular.

My biggest bugbear is when the air-con is set too low. I've stayed in hotels that purport to be eco while their air-conditioning blasts freezing air wherever you go. There have been some great advancements in eco-air-cons, for example, sea-water air-conditioning (SWAC) which uses a nearby cold-water source and saves more than 90 per cent of the energy used for conventional air conditioning.

We all have blind spots and secret guilty pleasures – personally I love nothing more than a big, deep bath and I'm wincing at how many showers I've kept running until they are the right temperature. However, thinking of the strain it puts on local utilities helps you think twice.

"

> A small rural village might use just a few hundred litres of water a month while the fancy hotel next door churns through a couple of thousand litres a night.

"

Each shower uses around 50 litres of water and baths can require a few hundred, not to mention a possible diesel-powered generator required to desalinate the water. So, try to stick to a quick splash – enough to wash your hair, with the water off between rinses. Many hotels will give instructions for where to hang your towels if you don't want to send them to the laundry each day, which is another easy way to cut down your water usage.

Be low-maintenance

I'm more than fine with reusing my sheets and towels – I'm told by hoteliers that British people usually are – but the truly green will often refuse all housekeeping services. This is a great way to conserve energy, but on the other hand, if everyone went Do Not Disturb on the house-keeping, someone who really needs the work could be out of a job. It depends on the context, how they run their operations, and where in the world you are – if you being more self-sufficient translates as having a lighter touch on natural resources, that's a green light that you're being greener. If you're in a country where wages are likely to be low and letting someone have a sweep around is part of their job and it gives you a reason to subsidise their mea-gre earnings through a tip, think of yourself as supporting the social impact through the service provided, or make some noise if they don't.

And I know the complimentary toiletries can be tempting, but as soon as you open them they'll be replaced with yet more mini plastic bottles. So do your bit to reduce waste and instead bring your own or check they lay things on via refillable dispensers.

Minimise waste

Zero plastic is always a worthy target, but it's especially important in places without municipal waste management or where rubbish might end up in nature. I often take a little extra bag with me to places where picking up a little litter as you walk is helpful. At Bambu Indah in Bali, owner John Hardy sets off every day at 7am on his trash walk at this remarkable riverside retreat. And you don't even need to stay in one of their open-air love shacks overlooking rice paddy fields or the Ayung River to talk rubbish with the founder of the Green School. As you walk along spearing garbage with a bamboo pole, sarong-wearing John is not shy when it comes to pointing out how we could all be living greener lives.

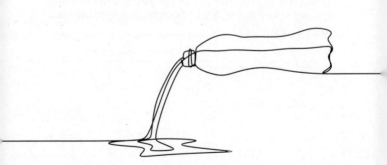

FOOD
CHOICES

Consuming hyper-local and seasonal products which don't involve loads of packaging is always the ideal. Skip anywhere with buffets, as these generate large amounts of food waste, most of which ends up in landfill. (In this new germaphobic era, they're also distinctly out of fashion.)

As we covered in previous sections, don't buy bottled water if it is safe to drink from the tap. If you prefer the taste of mineral water, many establishments have their own in-house sanitary filtration and bottling system which serves highest-quality still and sparkling.

If you're a carnivore, flex some flexitarian ways and swerve emissions-creating meat on the menu if you can — the holy grail is homegrown veg-based dishes. And if you do end up eating meat, try to avoid beef, which is a far higher contributor to environmental harm. If you've watched any of the glut of shows from *Food, Inc.* to *What the Health*, whether you agree with their narratives or not, they lift the lid on big agriculture, exposing how industrial-scale farming puts profit well before health, small producers, animals and the environment.

TRAVELLING
AS A VEGAN OR
VEGETARIAN

As talk of the evils of plastic have finally hit the mainstream, plant-based lifestyles have been peaking, too.

However, it's often a challenge for vegans and vegetarians to find somewhere that not only looks lovely but also caters to their culinary preferences.

'What use are beautiful rooms and enticing pools when all you can order in the restaurant are the side dishes?' says Thomas Klein, founder of Veggie Hotels. Their directory helps to steer those who don't want to compromise their diets when staying away from home, whatever their particular needs. It's understandable that those trying to lead more sustainable lives may favour a plant-based diet, since meat-based food systems require more energy, land, and water resources than typical lacto-ovo vegetarian diets (including eggs and dairy). An Oxford study in 2018 revealed a quarter of all greenhouse gas emissions come from food production, supporting a belief that meat options produce more greenhouse gases than meat-free sources chosen by vegans.

However, just like all aspects of sustainability, how to be greener through what we eat and drink is a nuanced topic. The same study revealed that the process of producing one glass of dairy milk emits almost three times the greenhouse gases of a non-dairy alternative, yet making almond 'milk' requires a staggering 74 litres of water. A vegan diet can also increase demand for plants like soya, which need to be imported. So it's important, whatever our diets, to consider our 'food miles' as a measure of from plant to plate (see 'foodprint', page 129).

ACTIVITIES

Choosing experiences where we get to have a great time without compromising the wellbeing of other people or the planet is the goal — and the ideal is when we are able to give back more than we receive through all that we do while we're away.

Are watersports a threat to marine life?

There are varying degrees of impact depending on the activity, and location. Any human behaviour that affects the quality of life for inhabitants of the ocean is obviously not good. But thanks to many organisations, awareness and initiatives abound, and judiciously chosen watersports can actually support ocean conservation.

Diving and snorkelling can cause damage to sensitive marine ecosystems, such as coral reefs – so choose operators with a Green Fins initiative seal of approval from the United Nations Environment Programme (UNEP). Noise from adrenaline sports may disrupt acoustic communication, so eschewing jet skis and loud motorboats is no doubt kinder to marine life. The motion of boating isn't all we should consider, also think about the chemicals used to clean watercraft which leach into the water.

66

The Outdoor Swimming Society proposes a code of conduct that urges all wild swimmers to consider our impact on fishing folk, boaters, nesting birds and, of course, asks us to take away our rubbish and any we find along the way.

99

Indigenous insight

Indigenous or tribal peoples are a vital part of our history and carry the wisdom of numerous epochs of life on Earth. They make up only 5 per cent of the world's population but are estimated to care for around a quarter of the world's land and 80 per cent of its biodiversity. Yet their role has never been so under threat – these communities are most at risk from dramatic climate change and a freeze on wealth distribution. Historically vilified for refusing to assimilate to the ways of invading settlers, to this day they are often still treated as second-class citizens, criticised for falling by the wayside rather than adopting the incompatible ways of newcomers. It's horrifying.

Indigenous people carry an intuition and insight into nature that is like a superpower. Their knowledge around the unimaginable healing power of plants is something the Big Pharma world work hard to discredit. We could all learn from more time spent with indigenous people, and any travel services that help preserve their lifestyles and provide revenue in a way that lets them maintain their heritage should be supported.

Joining indigenous people as guides or taking a workshop with them is a great way to ensure your holiday gives something back – and, of course, it makes for a more enriching overall experience. Who better to show you around a neighbourhood than someone who is born and bred there? At the Royal Botanic Gardens in Sydney, you can join an Aboriginal Heritage Tour with a member of the Gadigal tribe. It illustrates these natives' ingenuity in action, and they offer practical insights such as how paperbark can be used to wrap food, or how candlenuts can be soaked then eaten or used for their multi-purpose oil. In Sri Lanka, I was once able to spend time with the chief of the last of the Vedda people. Working with a translator, I got a sense of his off-the-scale knowledge spanning the medicinal properties of so many plants.

Can playing golf ever be green?

Crazy amounts of water are needed to keep typical fairway grasses match-fit, which is especially challenging in dry parts of the world. So seek out more organic greens. Consider those that use environmentally friendly fertilisers and cunning watering systems. Look out for a resort that has EarthCheck's seal of approval, thanks to having added treatment plants to process the waste water generated from the resort and its surrounding community to do all the fairway watering.

Beach cleaning

Organise or attend a beach clean — especially since our shorelines and seas have never been so trashed as they are now from single-use plastic. Consult the Marine Conservation Society or Surfers Against Sewage to find out how to help care for the coastlines.

SOUVENIRS AND KEEPSAKES

In the past, most of what we saw, touched, tasted or bought overseas was different to what we knew at home, and because of that trinkets and keepsakes were interesting at every turn. Now, wherever you might be in the world, they could have been made in China. Locally made products and local businesses should always be favoured. While natural materials are usually better than synthetic, it's always worth asking questions about the origin of the materials to ensure they have been grown or harvested responsibly. Things made using ivory, tortoisehell or horn are obviously a no-no, as are coral, conch shells, rare hardwoods or skins, feathers or bones of wild animals.

A word on haggling: yes, it's part of many cultures, but I always cringe at wheeler-dealer tourists who take it too far. Remember, you could be bargaining a stallholder out of a pittance that they rely on to feed their family. If you think a seller is overcharging, consider asking for a better deal if you buy more.

RESPECTING LOCAL WILDLIFE AND MARINE ENVIRONMENTS

Anything that goes by a name that involves the word 'wild' wants to stay just that. Any alteration to the natural behaviour of wild creatures just isn't cool. Many years ago, I was invited to a cheetah 'sanctuary' in South Africa. We were encouraged to stroke a big cat, yet it had a considerable chain holding it down and we had to sign endless disclaimer forms for the 'privilege'. It is inconceivable to do such a thing today. Likewise, I remember as a kid thinking how glamorous it seemed to ride decorated elephants on holiday in India. But their spines can't support our weight and being made to carry humans causes serious spinal injuries. Also, those jingly-jangly howdah chairs give them painful blisters that are prone to infection. Not so jolly after all. It's the same story when it comes to marine life. A scuba diver may brag that they know how to coax in photo-worthy sharks, but it's probably by 'chumming' the water, a process of swishing bloody fishy bits around. Yuck and yikes.

HOW TO RESPECT
WILDLIFE ON
YOUR TRIP

---

*When it comes to other living species,
aim for saving, conserving, preserving
or admiring from afar.*

- Never feed or touch wildlife.

- Research the credentials of anywhere that is charging you for animal encounters. (See the discussion of zoos and aquariums, page 78.)

- Do not disturb natural environments, whether on land or in water. Make sure your presence doesn't cause damage to marine life, such as surfing with toxic sunscreen on, or by brushing coral reefs with flippers (see page 106).

- Keep beaches, riverbanks and animal habitats clean and safe for wildlife by picking up and disposing carefully of any rubbish that you see.

We need to strike it right when offering our time, so that we're genuinely helping those in need.

RESPONSIBLE VOLUNTEERING AND CHARITY WORK

We need to strike it right when offering our time, so that we're genuinely helping those in need. Volunteering needs to be suited to that specific culture – it's not just an outing to offer some virtue-signalling for social media. It may seem like a great idea to muck in at an orphanage, but if you're not qualified in childcare or a teacher with experience, you wouldn't be able to do that back home – so why there?

"

A stream of strangers is unlikely to be doing the children good if they're ogled like goldfish in a bowl.

"

If you have skills to impart or professional services to contribute, that's different. There are agencies that organise trips to place volunteers in projects where they can really be of help. (See volunteering holidays, page 64.)

Charitable giving

Whether they are cute children or desperate-looking adults, it is best not to give indiscriminately to beggars. It's good to avoid cultivating a culture of dependency or encouraging this as an alternative to school. As well-intentioned as charitable donations are, randomly handing out 'stuff', such as clothing, toys or sweets, to villagers and their children in rural communities can also create community conflict. Instead, you might want to give nutritious food to those in need, or support relevant charities.

TECHNOLOGY: DISCONNECT TO RECONNECT

It may not seem as though it has anything to do with being green, but releasing yourself from your phone when travelling will help you relate better to the humans you meet along the way.

Learn a few words in the language – even just 'hello' and 'thank you' – and the rewards are manifold. If you're staying in a city, dial down your data roaming and look up and around you – it feels good. If you're still using your smartphone as your guide, but going off-grid, before you leave your hotel lounge or lobby, log on to an app such as Citymapper to figure out the most efficient route. Better not to add to the handset zombies roaming the paths and pavements – instead of being glued to your phone, smile at passers-by. You may find going slow with an old-school map is better for giving you a more genuine sense of the lay of the land. While you're riding the subway or bus, deep-dive into some destination-relevant literature. Reading Rabindranath Tagore's short stories while in India or John Irving's novels in New England will be more enriching than scrolling any digital feed.

THE CONVERSATION CHALLENGE

When you are in new or exotic places, rather than spending precious time poking at your smartphone, striking up meaningful exchanges with others is an excellent way to encourage more positivity. (Depending on where you are – in Japan it's frowned upon to speak to strangers on the subway.) In the eighteenth century, coffee houses were filled with the fizz of big ideas and real social discourse; today, you'll probably just hear the phrase 'Can I get your wifi password?'

Maybe it's because conversation requires mental effort and turning to tech is easier than engaging in real-time, flesh-and-blood interactions. Chatting to strangers has become a bit weird and awkward for some, so they elect to have their ears occupied with the familiar through headphones instead. So I am laying down a challenge: strive for a deeper discourse with your friends and family while you're away.

Seek out meaningful exchanges with locals, not just other travellers, and listen, listen, listen. Travel is a wonderful opportunity to speak with people from different cultures, but time away is not only a time to observe and celebrate our differences, but to better understand our common humanity, and appreciate our similarities as people.

ON-THE-GO
ACTIVISM

*Pester power isn't just a kids' tactic.
When you're on the move, give friendly
feedback to businesses as to how they
can be more sustainable.*

As a travel writer and hotel reviewer, this has been part of my job for a long time. I recently asked a manager about their use of Fiji water in plastic bottles in a fancy restaurant in Spain. A month later, I discovered that they'd ditched the shipped stuff and replaced it with a nice-tasting local alternative in refillable glass containers. A victory for a little whispered activism.

Charm helps. Giving feedback to hotels about their small, plastic, bathroom toiletries in the spirit of free consultancy rather than complaint is preferable.

"

Imagine being the recipient of
whatever it is you are saying and
consider how you might respond.

"

You want whoever you are speaking to to take heed and listen, so ideally don't just present a problem but suggest a solution. Not everyone's a fan of the 'compliment sandwich', but it can be useful: start with a pleasantry and end on a positive, and put the negative message in between. Imply that it's a small thing but it could make a massive difference. It's an exercise in seeing things from the service provider's point of view and appreciating that they too might be frustrated by the challenge you've spotted.

For example: 'We had a lovely stay, but I think that your guests would really appreciate it if you could offer an alternative to those small, disposable plastic toiletries, such as refillable dispensers, and perhaps it could benefit you in other ways, such as reducing your waste. I hope this is helpful feedback'.

GLOSSARY

CHAPTER 3

A-Z OF GREEN TRAVEL TERMS

Understanding the key terms and meanings of language associated with every aspect of sustainability will empower you to seek out those services and products which have exceptionally green credentials and navigate you through the greenwash to plan and experience the most eco-friendly escapes.

ACCESSIBILITY

Support travel services and hosts that allow everyone to have the fullest experiences, regardless of ability, age, gender or sexuality. Encouraging inclusivity means that more people will be able to have quality travel experiences. Tourists who have accessibility issues simply want to enjoy the same holiday as the next person.

AMENITIES

These are the extras to which hospitality treats us or thinks we might like or need. The problem is that it often means disposable and single-use plastic junk. What are the alternatives? Refillable pump dispensers made locally for all-natural paraben-free products are increasingly used instead of miniatures.

ANIMAL WELFARE

Sorry, no riding elephants or cuddling koalas for photos, folks. There's a reason why wildlife is called 'wild'. If we could ask animals if they'd prefer to exist as nature intended, my guess is that they'd say yes. So back off and enjoy them from a distance without disturbing them.

BIODIVERSITY

This is the complexity of life on Earth, in all its forms. In the natural world, every ecosystem is perfectly balanced to work in harmony towards our planet's overall health.

BIOPHILIA

Meaning a love of nature, and our innate connection to it. Inspired by natural surroundings and all things living, biophilic design recreates nature's idiosyncratic patterns and biological forms in architecture and interiors.

CARBON EMISSIONS

Greenhouse gases are mostly comprised of carbon dioxide, and that's why we conflate carbon with the likes of nitrous oxide and methane. The increasing volume of carbon dioxide and its friends in the atmosphere is essentially wrapping the planet in a blanket, causing it to warm up. Tourism is guilty of spewing out about 10 per cent of the world's total emissions.

CARBON FOOTPRINT
This refers to the total greenhouse gases produced by an individual or business, represented in tonnes of carbon dioxide. Flying is the single biggest contributor to our footprints and it's the taking off and landing parts that cause the highest emissions. While travelling, skip internal flights in favour of public transport, trains in particular, and walk everywhere you can. Staying in energy-efficient hotels and following a plant-based diet helps, too.

CARBON NEUTRAL
This is when businesses measure the amount of carbon they're responsible for releasing, and they balance it out with an equivalent amount of 'credits'. This involves negative emissions being calculated and then the right amount of activity invested in to absorb the equivalent amount of carbon, to offset.

CARBON OFFSETTING
It's important to check your offsetting money is heading in the right direction (see page 72). A recent study by the European Commission found that 85 per cent of the offset projects used by the EU under the UN's Clean Development Mechanism failed to reduce emissions.

CARBON POSITIVE
When a building or activity produces more energy than it uses. Less than zero carbon emissions is the goal for many businesses – but it's easier aimed for than achieved.

CERTIFICATIONS

Official accreditations from third-party assessments signify an operator has conformed to a standard of practice. EarthCheck, BREEAM and LEED denote green building principles (see page 51). B Corp's accredited businesses are legally required to consider the impact of all their decisions on their workers, customers, suppliers, community and the environment.

CIRCULAR ECONOMY

Traditionally, industry follows a linear take–make–waste system where natural resources are plundered to produce something which is sold, used, then disposed of. In nature, there's no such thing as waste – think about how organisms process nutrients and their excretions then become matter useful to another phase in the system. It's a beautiful zero-waste thing. In terms of travel, it can refer to operations that aren't wasteful and where supply chains are resourceful, ethical and transparent.

CITIZEN SCIENCE

Data collection can be the most time-consuming part of conservation, so contributing to projects in this way is as green as can be. Volunteers using the iNaturalist app can upload photos of animals and plants, which identifies the species, and thus help to map out biodiversity and contribute to Forestry England's Big Forest Find, the country's largest survey of forest wildlife.

CLOSED LOOP

A system inspired by nature (as many of the best ideas are) where things are reused again and again. A virtuous circle sees goods reused or repurposed and put back into the economy, rather than following a traditional approach to procurement that involves buying goods, using them, then disposing of them. It can refer to organic leftovers composted by a restaurant in which to grow its ingredients. And on it goes.

COMPOSTING

The biggest contributor to landfills globally is food waste, which never gets the chance to be re-invested in the environment. The 'rot' in our sustainability 'R's – our leftovers and food scraps – make the ideal natural, eco-friendly fertiliser.

CONSERVATION

Promoting ecosystems with integrity is the name of this game. While protecting natural resources and safeguarding biodiversity, it's also about educating everyone on responsible management of energy, water and waste, land planning and the dynamic between animals and nature.

DRAWDOWN

This refers to the ideal point when levels of greenhouse gases in the atmosphere stop climbing and start declining. Project Drawdown is the non-profit organisation working towards this goal.

DRINKING WATER

The truth is that tap water is often fine. For when it's not, praise be to any business with an in-house bottling plant so they can serve sparkling and still water in reusable glass bottles, removing the need for anything imported: water or plastic. You can also buy water purification tablets to carry with you when you're on the move.

FOODPRINT

The ecological impact of food, from production to waste. Harvesting, refrigeration, continent-hopping, cooking, leftovers – producing food means methane and GHG emissions, especially if it's discarded and left to find its way to landfill. Local and seasonal plant-based diets have a lower foodprint.

GREENHOUSE GASES (GHGS)

The greenhouse effect is caused by a build-up of greenhouse gases in the Earth's atmosphere; these include carbon dioxide (CO_2), methane (CH_4), nitrogen oxide (N_2O), ozone (O_3), fluorinated gases also known as chlorofluorocarbons (CFCs) and water vapour (H_2O).

GREYWATER

Waste water from sinks, showers and laundries, which is relatively clean and can be diverted for use in irrigation and flushing toilets.

GUERRILLA HUMANITARIANISM
Jon Rose from Waves For Water introduced me to this expression, and defined it as taking a no-nonsense, stripped-down approach to determining the essentials needed to complete a task. 'Sometimes, it's best to take matters into your own hands, bringing a solution directly to a problem, under the radar and around the red tape.'

HANDPRINT
The good we do (as opposed to our footprint). So, thank you for reading this book – if you act on some of what you are reading, that will give you a bigger handprint and a smaller footprint.

HOMESTAYS
When foreigners stay in locals' homes, resulting in authentic, immersive experiences, with the added benefit of direct-action wealth distribution to a household in an underprivileged area.

HYPERLOCAL
From snacks to souvenirs to furnishings, it's all about the provenance – always try to pick products from right where you are. And remember to take your reusable bag so you can decline any offered by the seller!

INDIGENOUS PEOPLE
Help the original people of a place, or the longest-term residents, celebrate their distinct linguistic, cultural and social characteristics. Preserving the culture of indigenous groups is immeasurably valuable and it helps improve their socio-economic conditions, alleviates poverty and inequality, and protects the environment.

INVASIVE SPECIES
Non-native plants that have been introduced to an environment and caused environmental or economic damage, or harm to human health.

NATURAL CLEANING PRODUCTS
The use of non-toxic and plant-based bathroom or kitchen products that are biodegradable and ethical are desirable in a place with a greener manifesto. More housekeeping departments are now staying spick and span by using old-fashioned vinegar or lemon juice, rather than phosphate-loaded detergents.

OFF-GRID
This can mean somewhere that's offline or a self-sufficient host that avoids municipal main utilities thanks to harnessing its own supply of power through renewable energy.

PAINT
Environmentally friendly, low-VOC paints are low in volatile organic compounds. Guests can breathe easier knowing that they are sleeping in a non-toxic room. It also means that those who applied the paint were not exposed to carcinogenic chemicals. Benzene and formaldehyde can be among the toxic chemicals found in traditional emulsions.

PERMACULTURE
Simply put, this is designing an ecosystem that mimics nature-based principles. It is based on working with nature not against it, from growing food to planning a garden to producing rich soil and achieving zero-waste status.

PLASTIC
We've seen the bottle-strewn beaches and PET-clogged ocean waters, and we've gasped at reports of microplastics now pumping through our bloodstreams or being present in newborns. Yet we're addicted to stuff made from it. Until we all take a stand and say no thanks to those eco-unfriendly sachets, sewing kits, shower caps and shrink-wrapped, toxic, pre-pasted toothbrushes, they will keep on coming. Since 90 per cent of plastic used is brand new and produced using fossil fuels, and with 8 per cent of all the world's extracted oil going towards plastic production, we shouldn't just offset airmiles but all the petrochemical-generated extras, too.

PROVENANCE
This term relates to the origin of everything from food to furniture, spanning all that you see, taste, touch and use. It considers quality, transparency, trust and traceability. A respect for provenance promotes all things seasonal, handmade and not industrially created.

RECYCLING
Any business or individual who strives to recycle, repurpose and reuse however and whatever they can, mindful of not being wasteful, is scoring big green points.

RENEWABLE ENERGY
Renewables – also referred to as green or clean energy – are generated from natural resources that never run out, such as solar rays, wind or water, as opposed fossil fuels such as coal, oil or natural gas.

REVERSE-OSMOSIS
A filtration treatment where water is processed by water molecules being forcibly passed through a semipermeable membrane – it can be used to desalinate seawater to create drinking water or to cleanse waste water.

REWILDING

This is not just about letting gardens grow wild, it can mean the reintroduction of plant or animal species into a habitat from which they have disappeared in order to boost biodiversity or restore the health of an ecosystem. To better understand this process, read George Monbiot's *Feral: Rewilding the Land, Sea and Human Life*; Robert Macfarlane's *Underland*; and Isabella Tree's *Wilding: The Return of Nature to a British Farm*.

SANITISED TRAVEL

One symptom of a pandemic-altered world is the emergence of cleanliness accreditations. Take a moment to consider what some of these guarantees of highest-level sanitisation and health checks at every touchpoint (excuse the pun) might mean. As the holistically minded eco traveller knows, lashings of disinfectant and chemicals to kill all bacteria unilaterally is probably not great for our individual immune systems or the health of the planet. Favour eco-friendly, naturally clean environments that allow good bacteria and biodiversity to flourish and which don't rely on lots of disposable-plastic goods. The post-COVID-19 obsession with hygiene has also led to a huge spike in throw-away personal protective equipment (PPE) and single-use products and wrapping ending up in waterways, so it is best to be even more mindful of minimising our contribution.

SHARING ECONOMY

Consumers' ability to borrow or rent things instead of buying, or when folks swap services or assets, either gratis or for a fee. Some of the best-known marketplaces based on this principle (Airbnb is an example) often have their origins in Silicon Valley, so it's more about capitalist ambitions than old-fashioned bartering.

SLOW TRAVEL

With an emphasis on living in harmony with nature, Carlo Petrini created the Slow Food Movement in Piedmont, Italy, as a protest against a McDonald's opening in Rome. Just as this movement celebrates local farming, regional cuisine, communal meals and traditional recipes, if we apply this to travel we see that it's not just about the pace, it's about being more mindful and making deeper connections with people, places and things.

STAKEHOLDERS

Individuals or groups that have an interest in or are affected by any decision or activity, particularly from a business.

UNDERTOURISM

This concept is about visiting under-the-radar places that will benefit from your visit because they're low profile or have experienced a dramatic drop in visitors, which in turn means a detrimental drop in income for residents of that community.

VEGAN TRAVEL

With many people now prioritising plant-based diets, it's logical that travellers with specific dietary requirements and preferences want to plan trips where they know they'll be catered for. Sleep, shower and savour a decent bit of sustenance free of animal products – that's not so much to ask for from a place to stay.

VFM

Historically, this stands for 'value for money' – the main influencing factor on people's purchasing decisions. It's great when you see more people caring about values than money when choosing how to holiday. How we assess the true meaning of value is ever-evolving. For me, it's about natural beauty, somewhere that pays its humans properly and invests in locally made furnishings.

VOLUNTOURISM

Working holiday packages may appear a noble way for us to help conserve wildlife or provide aid after a humanitarian disaster, but they aren't always useful. Scrutinise whether a situation is being exploited for commercial reasons, and question whether foreigners being parachuted in for a short burst or doing jobs that locals could be doing is in fact a negative.

WASTE

Back-of-house activity with integrity can set one hotel apart from another: those reducing the quantity of solid waste that goes to landfill thanks to an anaerobic digester or stringent recycling are greener. Even better if they're using it to produce biogas or biofertiliser.

Then there are the businesses in places where governments don't provide waste management, so they're starting green revolutions. Soneva doesn't only invest in 'waste-to-wealth' systems in their properties, but they're working hard to raise awareness around the negative impact of open burning of waste throughout the Maldives. They've even developed a scheme for the government that can be rolled out, the Namoona Baa Initiative. At the eco-centro complex they alchemise metals, bottles and coconut husks into items of economic value, such as eco-friendly building materials or compost.

WATER

An important consideration when you are away from home is whether you're a burden on local utilities – especially in places where water is in limited supply. Holidaymakers splash about in a lot more water than locals, with gallons pumped to operate resorts, pools and golf courses, particularly in tropical regions. So, it's good to know if your hosts manage water as a shared public resource or whether they are recklessly tapping into a supply that suits them best at the expense of others. There's much to consider; are you heading to a desert island where seawater needs to be desalinated using diesel generators? A good indicator of whether or not a hotel's a good guy is when they've created their own supply, such as a borehole for extracting water rather than depriving locals of their municipal water.

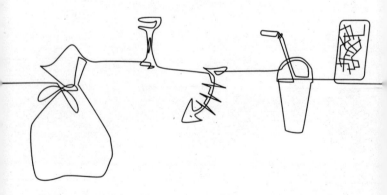

ZERO WASTE

The holy grail is sending nothing to landfill. Rubbish is never the sexiest subject, but honouring the tenets of sustainability – reducing our reliance on stuff; reusing, recycling and repurposing all we can; and prioritising a closed loop in terms of supply – is important.

ADDRESS BOOK

CHAPTER 4

BLUE BADGE STYLE

Arbiters of accessibility and hosts of the Blue Badge Access Awards (BBAAs), they celebrate the bars, restaurants, hotels, and entertainment and events venues, mostly in the UK, that are excellent for people with disabilities or special access requirements.

bluebadgestyle.com
bluebadgeaccessawards.com

BLUE VENTURES

A reputable agency that works with marine research teams in the field, in conjunction with local communities. Their expeditions in Madagascar, Belize and Timor-Leste have paved the way for some of the world's most ambitious, community-based marine conservation initiatives and spawned models for conservation and community empowerment that build resilience among some of the most vulnerable coastal communities and marine ecosystems in the world. This innovative and rewarding tourism model provides reliable income directly to local communities, reduces the reliance on fishing, enables capacity building and training, and enables them to make robust commitments.

blueventures.org

BORN FREE

This charity opposes the exploitation of wild animals in captivity and campaigns to keep them wild. They promote compassionate conservation to enhance the survival of threatened species in the wild and protect natural habitats, while respecting the needs and safeguarding the welfare of individual animals.

bornfree.org.uk

BOUTECO

This is my own independent online platform that steers style-conscious travellers to the best sustainable design-led hotels. I recommend hotels that I know to have big hearts, which I also think have great taste when it comes to their interiors and design. I also share inspiring stories of sustainability on Instagram as @BoutecoHotels. *bouteco.co*

CANOPY & STARS

This glamping booking website is a thoughtfully curated collection of treehouses, shepherd's huts, yurts and dog-friendly holidays in the UK. *canopyandstars.co.uk*

THE CONSCIOUS TRAVEL FOUNDATION

Set up during the Covid-19 pandemic, in response to the devastating impact on the hospitality industry worldwide, TCTF is a collective of travel businesses which aim to educate the industry and customers about how to travel better, helping us to use our travels to support high-impact conservation and community projects. *theconscioustravelfoundation.com*

EARTH CHANGERS

Connecting you with pioneering people and places which ensure extraordinary experiences that have a positive impact, Earth Changers leads you to the stars of responsible tourism.

earth-changers.com

EARTHCHECK

A respected organisation that guides travel businesses globally to validate their carbon claims and advises on their sustainability initiatives.

earthcheck.org

ETHICAL SHOPPING GUIDE

Check and compare the ethical creds of many brands as organised in product-specific categories including travel, fashion, food and drink, through the website.

thegoodshoppingguide.com

FRIENDS OF THE EARTH

Driving campaigns on issues including climate change, pollution, nuclear technology, genetic engineering, deforestation, pesticides, food and agriculture and economic policy, it's the world's largest grassroots environmental network. Their campaigners and lawyers to local groups and supporters push for systemic change.

friendsoftheearth.uk

G ADVENTURES

This adventure travel company founded by Canadian entrepreneur Bruce Poon Tip in 1990 offers hundreds of itineraries which engage and support local communities and social enterprises all over the world. Alongside running affordable small-group land, sea and river tours across all seven continents Planeterra Foundation is their sister non-profit organisation.

gadventures.com

INTREPID GROUP

Comprising four responsible tour-operator brands united by the vision of 'changing the way people see the world', in 2018 Intrepid Travel become the world's largest travel business to be certified B Corp. The Intrepid Foundation has raised millions of Australian dollars for more than 125 charities around the world by matching traveller donations dollar-for-dollar.

intrepidgroup.travel

IUCN

The International Union for the Conservation of Nature is the global authority on the status of the natural world and the measures needed to safeguard it. They publish the most authoritative assessment of the status of species through their 'red list' and they believe that the loss of species and decrease in biodiversity along with climate change are the greatest challenges facing humanity.

iucn.org

THE LEAP

Taking gap yearers, midlifers and corporates on volun-tourism escapes in South America, Africa and Asia, and volunteering their manual labour for the greater good.
theleap.co.uk

LIFESTRAW

These innovative straw products have a microbiological, membrane microfilter which allows you to access safe drinking water wherever you go. LifeStraw also runs a pro-gramme that ensures for every product purchased, a school child receives safe water for an entire academic year.
lifestraw.com

THE LONG RUN

Members of this non-profit programme include some of the world's most committed and passionate conserva-tionists, lodges, retreats and parks, guided by the 4Cs: Culture, Community, Conservation and Commerce.
thelongrun.org

MUCH BETTER ADVENTURES

A travel company for those who want to protect the world's wildest places through properly managed tourism. Five per cent of revenue goes to projects that help boost biodiversity and remove carbon from the atmosphere.
muchbetteradventures.com

NOMADNESS TRAVEL TRIBE

The mission of this collective of over 20,000 black and brown nomads set up by Evita Robinson, aims to show the world that travel has no racial, gender, religious, economic or interest limitations.

nomadnesstv.com

NOW FORCE FOR GOOD ALLIANCE

A collection of hotels that have a genuine commitment to sustainability, raising the bar on accountability and transparency around sustainability.

itmustbenow.com

PACK FOR A PURPOSE

Working with resorts and charities around the world, this American non-profit encourages travellers to take much-needed goods to support better welfare, health, education, animal welfare, and socioeconomic development, through donations in their end destination – what you pack depends on where you are going.

packforapurpose.org

PEBBLE MAGAZINE

A digital lifestyle hub dedicated to helping you live a greener life, recommending items from organic homewares through to ethical skincare.

pebblemag.com

REGENERATIVE TRAVEL
A global collection of independent boutique eco hotels.
regenerativetravel.com

RESPONSIBLE TRAVEL
An activist travel company arranges trips around the world which engage you with local people, their culture and their way of life, in a meaningful way that lets you enjoy the best of their environments with the least impact.
responsibletravel.com

THE SLOW CYCLIST
Small, expert-guided group cycling holidays in Transylvania, Tuscany, Zagori and Rwanda.
theslowcyclist.co.uk

STEPPES TRAVEL
With 30 years of experience planning tailor-made holidays and adventurous journeys from Antarctica to Asia, these responsible tour operators also have a Fund for Change: a collection of initiatives to promote sustainable travel and a 'call to arms' to the industry to take action.
steppestravel.com

SURFERS AGAINST SEWAGE

A beach-cleaning community which started its work protecting oceans, waves, beaches and wildlife in Cornwall; their #GenerationSea movement has grown into one of the most active environmental charities tackling plastic pollution.

sas.org.uk/take-action

TRAVELEYES

A tour operator founded by Amar Latif which specialises in serving blind as well as sighted travellers.

traveleyes-international.com

TREESISTERS

Through the planting of trees, this global network of women is working to accelerate the greening of our planet through feminine values, energy and leadership.

treesisters.org

UP NORWAY

Travel designers who invite you to plan and book authentic experiences so you can best experience Norway's cuisine, learn about their design or Viking ancestry to modern democracy, and get a sense of why their society, which is based on trust and equality, is considered one of the world's most sustainable.

upnorway.com

VEGANWELCOME

A web portal that lists recommended vegan-friendly hotels with scores of hotels, mostly in Europe, with a few in long-haul destinations.

vegan-welcome.com

VISIT NATIVES

Trips that support and embrace indigenous languages, cultures, beliefs, traditional dress and knowledge systems, with tours planned, designed and implemented by peoples such as the Maasai, the Hadzabe, and the Sami in Norway. Working with WINTA (World Indigenous Tourism Alliance), they follow the Indigenous Tourism Engagement Framework based on the United Nations' Declaration on the Rights of Indigenous Peoples, 2007, the Larrakia Declaration 2012.

visitnatives.com

WAVES FOR WATER

A charity founded by professional surfer, Jon Rose, it brings clean water to those in need and through their Clean Water Courier programme, travellers can purchase W4W filters and deliver them to destinations all over the world; they have programmes in countries such as Haiti, Indonesia, Liberia, Pakistan, Kenya, Brazil, Nicaragua, Afghanistan and Chile.

wavesforwater.org

WILD FRONTIERS

Off-the-track adventure tours, guided by the principles that their small group trips have a positive and sustainable social, economic and environmental impact.

wildfrontierstravel.com

THANK YOU

Thanks to my Manchester-born grandparents for irritating me throughout childhood with comments such as 'Be sure to rinse out and reuse that carrier bag. Where will all that plastic end up, otherwise?' I'm grateful for having a hard up but imagination-rich single mum, who unintentionally taught me the value of what you do have, not what you don't. And what would I do without my daughter keeping me in check and giving me hope for the next generation (she wags her finger at me if I buy a new pair of shoes, even from the charity shop)? I'm so grateful for friends and family who always encourage curious minds to think deeper, challenge the status quo and do the right thing.

Enormous thanks to all the many inspiring hoteliers who ripped up the rulebooks and let me join them on their journey and to those who've given me a platform for speaking my truths: Andrew at Cempedak; Arnaud, Piet and Mark at the Datai; Bob and Wilbert at UXUA; Soneva's Sonu and Eva; Claude for leading the way with The Sumba Foundation; Bill Bensley. Props to Zita Cobb, for making such an example of Fogo Island Inn and for making me blush with horror that I ever giggled at 'Newfie' jokes as a schoolkid in Canada. To Bali for luring me to meet Ronald Akili when Katamama first opened, and to John and Cynthia Hardy for giving me reason to spend my savings on sending my daughter to the Green School for a spell. Justin Wateridge at Steppes, for making grown-up chats about sustainable travel fun even when we were trying to be a serious audience for Prince Harry. To Mike McHugo and all the wonderful Education for All housemothers, who welcomed me and filmmaker Kuba Nowak into their boarding houses in Morocco and taught us an invaluable lesson about the importance of tourism in supporting the schooling of young women in remote rural areas. And to my beautiful godson Marko, for bringing home how important it is to give visibility to disability and how considering accessibility for all is another important aspect of sustainability. To those who've let me shout about what I care about: Melinda Stevens at Condé Nast Traveller magazine and to all those passionate about amplifying inspiring stories of sustainability, Mason Rose, Bird Travel PR, Fox Comms, Hue & Cry, Bacall PR, Joro Experiences, Helen Bagnall at Salon London, Also Festival, Indigoeight, Perowne International, Anna Nash at Aman, Sofie Askew, Emma Whitehair, Leah Whitfield, Emma Cripwell, Victoria Fuller, Pippa Ward, Hilary at Arlington Talent, James Jayasundera, Robert Elms on BBC Radio London and Tasha Self, who started as my intern many moons ago, and who has since gone on to become a precious perspective-broadening compadre.

To all the amazing people in hotels, shops and restaurants, who've patiently listened to my sustainability-related questions; and to the housekeeping and engineering folks who've answered my cross examinations. To Michelle Matthews, my travelling soulmate. To Melissa Hemsley – without you recommending me to Celia Palazzo after our poke around the waste management at Soneva Fushi, this book wouldn't exist. And the biggest thank you to everyone who cares enough to have read this book and to those who keep asking questions, keep being curious, keep up the critical thinking and keep caring. Above all, let's keep listening, thinking and talking.

INDEX

1

Ebury Press, an imprint of Ebury Publishing,
20 Vauxhall Bridge Road,
London, SW1V 2SA

Ebury Press is part of the Penguin Random House group of companies
whose addresses can be found at global.penguinrandomhouse.com

Penguin
Random House
UK

First published by Ebury Press in 2020
www.penguin.co.uk

A CIP catalogue record for this book is available from the British Library

Design: Louise Evans

ISBN: 978-1-529-10785-2

Printed and bound in Great Britain by Clays Ltd, Elcograf S.p.A.

Penguin Random House is committed to a sustainable future for
our business, our readers and our planet. This book is made from
Forest Stewardship Council® certified paper.